easy
BRITISH

THE AUSTRALIAN
Women's Weekly

contents

Cuisine is not the first thing we might associate with all things British – but where would we be without the traditional English breakfast, served the world over; try your hand at perfect roast beef with Yorkshire puddings of course; or look for something sweet amongst the desserts and puddings – a crumble, bread and butter pudding or a good old fashioned apple pie! For everything British from breakfast to dessert.

Food Director

Pamela Clark

breakfasts

boiled eggs

preparation time 5 minutes ▨ cooking time 5 minutes (plus cooling time)

1 Choose saucepan to suit the number of eggs you are boiling; one egg in small saucepan, up to four eggs in medium saucepan; more eggs in large saucepan (there should be enough room to move eggs around). Add enough cold water to cover eggs. Stir constantly using wooden spoon over high heat until water boils; this will centralise each yolk. Boil, uncovered, until yolks are as soft or as firm as you like. As a guide, 3 minutes will give you set egg white and soft yolk. After 5 minutes, the yolk will be set.
2 Place saucepan of eggs under cold running water about 1 minute or until eggs are cool. This will stop a dark ring forming around the yolk.
3 Serve boiled eggs with toast soldiers, if desired.

COOKING WITH EGGS
▨ Store eggs in refrigerator with ends pointing down so the yolk is less likely to break when egg is used. As eggshells are porous they should not be washed before storing or stored near strong-smelling foods.
▨ To shell hard-boiled eggs, remove from boiling water; crack shells all over and plunge into bowl of cold water to speed cooling process.
▨ Always use the freshest eggs possible.
▨ Before using eggs in a recipe, break one at a time into a small saucer, that way, a stale egg can be discarded, rather than ruin the whole dish.

tips to peel eggs, crack shells gently and leave eggs immersed in cold water for at least 5 minutes or until cold; remove shells, starting from broad end; wash eggs; pat dry using absorbent paper

SCRAMBLING EGGS

■ Scrambled eggs are simply eggs mixed with milk (or cream) and butter, then stirred gently until cooked to your personal taste. The eggs should be barely firm when cooked and creamy in texture. Be patient when cooking scrambled eggs; it is important to keep the heat low and even. If cooked too quickly the eggs will toughen, or if stirred too much they will separate with a fine crumbly texture floating in a watery substance – though they are still edible.

■ You need to use a medium heavy-base saucepan; thin pans transfer the heat too quickly to the eggs and tend to burn the mixture.

■ Use cream instead of milk for a richer result; thin pouring cream gives the best results.

■ Serve scrambled eggs straight away; they can't be reheated successfully.

herbed scrambled eggs

preparation time 5 minutes ▦ cooking time 5 minutes
▦ serves 2

6 eggs
½ cup (125ml) milk
1 tablespoon finely chopped
fresh flat-leaf parsley
1 tablespoon finely chopped
fresh chives
1 teaspoon butter

1 Lightly beat eggs in small bowl using whisk; whisk in milk
and herbs.
2 Melt butter in medium saucepan over low heat; add egg
mixture. When mixture begins to set on base of pan, gently fold
mixture over using wooden spoon so uncooked mixture runs to
base of pan. Continue to cook and fold gently until eggs are still
creamy and slightly firm.
3 Serve with english muffins, if desired.

▦ **microwave method** Complete step 1.
Place butter in shallow dish (we used a pie
plate). Melt on HIGH (100%) about 15 seconds.
Add egg mixture; cook on HIGH (100%) about
3 minutes or until barely firm. Gently fold egg
mixture over using wooden spoon twice during
cooking time.

bacon and eggs

preparation time 5 minutes ▧ cooking time 10 minutes
▧ serves 2

4 bacon rashers (280g)
1 tablespoon vegetable oil
4 eggs
1 medium tomato (190g), halved

1 Cook bacon in medium frying pan, uncovered, until
browned and cooked as desired. Remove from pan;
keep warm.
2 Place oil in pan; break eggs into pan or into greased
egg rings in pan. Cook, uncovered, until egg white has set
and yolk is cooked as desired.
3 Meanwhile, place tomato, cut-side up, onto baking
tray; season with salt and pepper, if desired. Place under
heated grill; cook tomato until browned lightly and just
tender.
4 Serve fried eggs, bacon and tomato with toast, if
desired.

FRYING EGGS

▧ Use a heavy-base frying pan;
the size doesn't matter. Gentle
cooking is the secret; use either
a little butter or oil in the pan,
a pan sprayed with non-stick
spray, or a pan with a non-stick
surface.

▧ Butter should be hot but
not browned when you add the
egg; if butter is too hot, the egg
will burn around the edge and
underneath before the centre is
cooked. Spoon a little hot oil or
butter over egg to help it cook.

▧ Some people prefer a fried
egg with a crispy base. To
attain this, increase the heat
carefully until the white is as
crisp as you like.

▧ Serve the egg immediately;
fried eggs do not reheat
successfully.

▧ Always choose the freshest
egg available so the white sets
in a good shape when cooked; a
stale egg will result in a watery
white when cooked.

corned beef hash with poached eggs

preparation time 10 minutes ▪ cooking time 10 minutes ▪ serves 2

1 medium brown onion (150g),
chopped finely
3 medium potatoes (600g), grated
500g cooked corned beef,
shredded
2 tablespoons finely chopped
fresh flat-leaf parsley
2 tablespoons plain flour
2 eggs, beaten lightly
1 tablespoon vegetable oil
4 eggs, extra

1 Combine onion, potato, beef, parsley, flour and egg in large
bowl; mix well.

2 Divide mixture into four portions; flatten to form patties.

3 Heat oil in large heavy-base frying pan; cook patties, uncovered,
until browned both sides and potato is tender.

4 Put a little butter or oil on index finger; grease inside egg rings
or spray lightly with non-stick spray. Place about 1cm water in
frying pan so egg will not be covered. Bring water to a boil; reduce
heat until water is barely simmering. Place rings into water; gently
pour extra eggs, one at a time, into rings.

5 Egg white will start to set. If eggs are large, a little white may
seem to puff up around top of rings. Make sure water doesn't
boil or white will toughen. Start spooning water over yolks until
set to taste. The time this takes will depend on type and size of
pan, amount and heat of water, size and temperature of eggs
and, most important, individual preference.

6 Carefully lift rings away from eggs; lift eggs from water using
egg slide. Serve hash patties topped with poached eggs; top with
shredded basil, if desired.

POACHING EGGS
▪ Poaching is a gentle method of cooking
food in simmering liquid. Eggs should be
lowered into simmering water that should
almost cover the eggs, not submerge them.
▪ The pan may be covered or uncovered.
When covered, the eggs are cooked by the
trapped steam as well as the simmering
water. When uncovered, the water can
be spooned over the top of the eggs until
cooked to suit your taste.

tips to top off a salad or serve
with a sauce, poached eggs make
for great eating

the classic way Boil water in saucepan. Stir water briskly using wooden spoon to cause a whirlpool, then gently lower the egg from a jug or cup into the centre of the whirlpool. Reduce heat so water is barely simmering, then cook the egg, covered or uncovered, as outlined on left. If you cover pan, start checking after 1 minute to see if the egg is done to your liking. If you don't cover pan, spoon the water gently over egg until the yolk is set to suit your taste.

microwave cooking you can also poach an egg in a microwave oven very effectively; the egg has a texture similar to an egg cooked in an electric or manual poaching appliance. Break an egg into an ordinary teacup (it is not necessary to grease the cup), prick the yolk using fork otherwise the yolk will burst during cooking. Microwave on HIGH (100%) about 30 seconds or until cooked as desired.

omelette with ham and cheese

preparation time 5 minutes ▪ cooking time 5 minutes ▪ serves 1

2 eggs

1 tablespoon water

2 teaspoons butter

1 tablespoon finely chopped
fresh chives

1 tablespoon small fresh basil
leaves

filling

1 small tomato (130g), halved,
deseeded

1 slice ham

¼ cup (30g) grated cheddar
cheese

1 Break eggs into medium bowl; add the water. Use fork or whisk to mix only until yolks and whites are blended.

2 Heat 20cm frying pan over high heat for about 1 minute. Add butter to pan; it should sizzle and foam immediately if pan is hot enough. Do not allow butter to brown. Tip pan so butter covers base and halfway up side evenly.

3 Pour egg mixture into hot pan; it should begin to set around edge of pan almost immediately. Use wooden spoon to pull edge of omelette away from side of pan, allowing running mixture to reach hot pan and cook. Omelette is cooked when egg mixture no longer runs freely, but top still looks creamy. Omelette should be only browned lightly underneath.

4 Spoon filling over half of the omelette, opposite handle; this way, it is easier to slide omelette onto plate when cooked. Use spatula to fold omelette in half, covering filling, and slide onto serving plate; serve omelette immediately, sprinkled with herbs.

▪ filling Cut tomato flesh into strips. Cut ham into strips. Combine tomato and ham in bowl with cheese; mix lightly.

Omelettes come in a variety of types; this is a basic omelette. The eggs are lightly beaten then cooked quickly over a fairly high heat; the omelette can be eaten with or without filling. It is important to work quickly or the egg mixture in contact with the sides and base of the pan will overcook and will brown and toughen; the finished omelette should only be lightly browned underneath. We used a fairly heavy aluminium omelette pan with a base measuring around 20cm.

porridge with rolled grains

1 Place grain and soaking
liquid in medium bowl, cover;
stand at room temperature
overnight.
2 Place undrained grain in
medium saucepan; cook,
stirring, until mixture comes
to a boil. Add cooking
liquid, reduce heat; simmer,
uncovered, for required
cooking time. Serve warm
with toppings of your choice.

We used water to make these porridges, but skimmed milk or various fruit
juices are an option, if desired. The amounts given below for each type of
porridge are enough to make 4 servings.

grain	amount	soaking liquid	cooking liquid	cooking time	makes
rolled rice	¾ cup (75g)	1½ cups (375ml)	¾ cup (180ml)	10 mins	1¾ cups
rolled barley	¾ cup (75g)	1½ cups (375ml)	¾ cup (180ml)	25 mins	1½ cups
rolled oats	¾ cup (60g)	1½ cups (375ml)	½ cup (125ml)	10 mins	1½ cups
rolled rye	¾ cup (75g)	1½ cups (375ml)	1½ cups (375ml)	50 mins	1¾ cups
rolled triticale*	¾ cup (75g)	1½ cups (375ml)	1½ cups (375ml)	45 mins	1¼ cups

*triticale is a rye/wheat hybrid grain available in health stores.

TOPPINGS

These toppings are enough
for a single serving of porridge.

½ cup (125ml) skimmed milk
1 teaspoon honey
1 tablespoon low-fat vanilla
yogurt
pinch cinnamon
½ mashed banana
1 tablespoon dried fruit
2 teaspoons toasted shredded
coconut

rolled barley

rolled rice

rolled rye

rolled triticale

rolled oats

soups

lamb and barley soup

preparation time 15 minutes ▓ cooking time 1 hour 25 minutes
▓ serves 6

1.5kg french-trimmed lamb
shanks
3 litres (12 cups) water
¾ cup (150g) pearl barley
1 medium carrot (120g),
sliced thinly
1 medium leek (350g),
sliced thinly
2 trimmed celery stalks
(200g), sliced thinly
1 tablespoon curry powder
250g trimmed swiss chard,
chopped coarsely

1 Combine lamb, the water and barley in large saucepan; bring to
a boil. Reduce heat; simmer, uncovered, 1 hour, skimming surface
and stirring occasionally. Add carrot, leek and celery; simmer,
uncovered, 10 minutes.
2 Remove lamb from soup mixture. When cool enough to handle,
remove meat; chop coarsely. Discard bones and any fat or skin.
3 Dry-fry curry powder in small saucepan until fragrant. Return
meat to soup with curry powder and swiss chard; cook, uncovered,
until silver beet wilts.

tips you need 1kg of untrimmed
swiss chard to get the amount required
for this recipe

scotch broth
with cheese scones

2.25 litres (9 cups) water
1kg lamb neck chops
¾ cup (150g) pearl barley
1 large brown onion (200g),
diced into 1cm pieces
2 medium carrots (240g),
diced into 1cm pieces
1 medium leek (350g), sliced
thinly
2 cups (160g) finely shredded
savoy cabbage
½ cup (60g) frozen peas
2 tablespoons coarsely chopped
fresh flat-leaf parsley

cheese scones
1 cup self-raising flour
pinch cayenne pepper
2 tablespoons finely grated
parmesan cheese
½ cup coarsely grated cheddar
½ cup milk

preparation time 30 minutes ▪ cooking time 1 hour 45 minutes
▪ serves 4

1 Place the water in large saucepan with lamb and barley; bring
to a boil. Reduce heat; simmer, covered, 1 hour, skimming fat
from surface occasionally. Add onion, carrot and leek; simmer,
covered, about 30 minutes or until carrot is tender.
2 Meanwhile, make cheese scones.
3 Remove lamb from pan. When cool enough to handle, remove
and discard bones; shred lamb coarsely.
4 Return lamb to soup along with cabbage and peas; cook,
uncovered, about 10 minutes or until cabbage is just tender.
5 Serve bowls of soup sprinkled with parsley, and accompanied
with scones.

▪ cheese scones Preheat oven to 220°C/200°C fan-assisted.
Lightly grease and flour 8cm x 26cm baking tin. Combine flour,
cayenne, parmesan and half the cheddar in medium bowl; pour in
milk, stir until mixture forms a sticky dough. Gently knead dough
on floured surface until smooth; use hand to flatten dough to
2cm-thickness. Using 4.5cm cutter, cut rounds from dough; place
rounds, slightly touching, in tin. Brush scones with a little milk then
sprinkle with remaining cheddar. Bake about 20 minutes.

cream of chicken soup

preparation time 35 minutes ▢ cooking time 2 hours 30 minutes
▢ serves 4

2 litres (8 cups) water
1 litre (4 cups) chicken stock
1.8kg whole chicken
1 medium carrot (120g), chopped coarsely
1 trimmed celery stalk (100g), chopped coarsely
1 medium brown onion (150g), chopped coarsely
40g butter
⅓ cup (50g) plain flour
2 tablespoons lemon juice
½ cup (125ml) cream
¼ cup finely chopped fresh flat-leaf parsley

1 Place the water and stock in large saucepan with chicken, carrot, celery and onion; bring to a boil. Reduce heat; simmer, covered, 1½ hours. Remove chicken from pan; simmer broth, covered, 30 minutes.

2 Strain broth through muslin-lined sieve or colander into large heatproof bowl; discard solids. Remove and discard chicken skin and bones; shred meat coarsely.

3 Melt butter in large saucepan, add flour; cook, stirring, until mixture thickens and bubbles. Gradually stir in broth and juice; bring to a boil, stirring. Add cream, reduce heat; simmer, uncovered, about 25 minutes, stirring occasionally. Add chicken; stir soup over medium heat until hot.

4 Serve soup sprinkled with parsley.

vegetable soup

preparation time 15 minutes
cooking time 35 minutes ▪ serves 4

1 tablespoon vegetable oil
2 large brown onions (400g), chopped finely
2 large carrots (360g), chopped coarsely
8 trimmed celery stalks (800g), chopped coarsely
3 cloves garlic, crushed
1 litre (4 cups) vegetable stock
1 litre (4 cups) water
¾ cup (165g) soup pasta
2 medium courgettes (240g), sliced thickly
250g trimmed swiss chard, chopped coarsely

1 Heat oil in large saucepan; cook onion, carrot, celery and garlic, stirring, until vegetables soften.
2 Add stock and the water; bring to a boil. Reduce heat; simmer, uncovered, 10 minutes. Add pasta and courgettes; simmer, uncovered, stirring occasionally, about 5 minutes or until pasta is tender. Add swiss chard; cook, stirring, until it just wilts.

tips you need approximately 1kg swiss chard for this recipe

potato and leek soup

preparation time 30 minutes (plus cooling time)
 cooking time 55 minutes serves 4

2 medium potatoes (400g), chopped coarsely

2 medium carrots (240g), chopped coarsely

1 large brown onion (200g), chopped coarsely

1 medium tomato (150g), chopped coarsely

1 trimmed celery stalk (100g), chopped coarsely

1.5 litres (6 cups) water

1 tablespoon olive oil

50g butter

4 medium potatoes (800g), chopped coarsely, extra

1 large leek (500g), sliced thickly

300ml cream

2 tablespoons finely chopped fresh chives

1 tablespoon finely chopped fresh basil

1 tablespoon finely chopped fresh dill

1 Combine potato, carrot, onion, tomato, celery and the water in large saucepan; bring to a boil. Reduce heat; simmer, uncovered, 20 minutes. Strain broth through muslin-lined sieve or colander into large heatproof bowl; discard solids.

2 Heat oil and butter in same cleaned pan; cook extra potato and leek, covered, 15 minutes, stirring occasionally. Add broth; bring to a boil. Reduce heat; simmer, covered, 15 minutes. Cool 15 minutes.

3 Meanwhile, make croûtons.

4 Blend or process soup, in batches, until smooth. Return soup to same cleaned pan, add cream; stir over medium heat until hot.

5 Serve bowls of soup sprinkled with combined herbs then topped with croûtons.

 croûtons Cut and discard crusts from 2 slices wholemeal bread; cut bread into 1cm pieces. Melt 50g butter in medium frying pan. Add bread; cook, stirring, until croûtons are browned lightly. Drain on absorbent paper.

cream of spinach soup

preparation time 20 minutes (plus cooling time) ▪ cooking time 35 minutes
▪ serves 6

40g butter
1 large brown onion (200g), chopped finely
2 cloves garlic, crushed
3 medium potatoes (600g), chopped coarsely
3 cups (750ml) chicken stock
1 litre (4 cups) water
250g trimmed spinach, chopped coarsely
¾ cup (180ml) cream

1 Melt butter in large saucepan; cook onion and garlic, stirring, until onion softens. Add potato, stock and water; bring to a boil. Reduce heat; simmer, covered, about 15 minutes or until potato is tender. Stir in spinach; cool 15 minutes.
2 Blend or process soup, in batches, until smooth. Return soup to same cleaned pan, add cream; stir over medium heat until hot.

tips for a delicious accompaniment, sprinkle slices of french bread stick with crumbled cheshire cheese and finely grated lemon rind; toast under a hot grill until lightly browned

carrot & lentil soup

preparation time 25 minutes
cooking time 55 minutes   serves 4

1.125 litres (4½ cups) vegetable stock
2 large brown onions (400g), chopped finely
4 cloves garlic, crushed
1 tablespoon ground cumin
6 large carrots (1kg), chopped coarsely
2 trimmed sticks celery (150g), chopped coarsely
2 cups (500ml) water
½ cup (100g) brown lentils
½ cup (125ml) buttermilk

1 Heat ½ cup (125ml) stock in large saucepan;
cook onion, half of the garlic and cumin, stirring,
until onion softens. Add carrot and celery; cook,
stirring, 5 minutes.
2 Add remaining stock and the water; bring to
a boil. Reduce heat; simmer, uncovered, about
20 minutes or until carrot softens.
3 Blend or process soup, in batches, until
smooth; return soup to pan. Add lentils; simmer,
uncovered, about 20 minutes or until lentils are
tender.
4 Stir buttermilk into hot soup and serve
immediately.

tips can be made 1 day ahead to
stage 3 and refrigerated, covered

fish & seafood

prawn and avocado cocktail

preparation time 15 minutes ■ serves 2

400g large cooked prawns
lettuce leaves
½ medium avocado (125g),
chopped coarsely
lemon wedges
4 chives, trimmed

cocktail sauce
½ cup (150g) mayonnaise
2½ tablespoons tomato sauce
¼ teaspoon worcestershire sauce
¼ teaspoon chilli sauce

1 Pinch heads from bodies of prawns. Peel shell away from centre of body, leaving tails intact.
2 Remove back veins by pulling veins from head end towards tail end.
3 Line serving dishes with lettuce leaves. Place prawns and avocado into dishes; spoon cocktail sauce over prawn mixture. Serve with lemon wedges and chives.

■ **cocktail sauce** Combine mayonnaise and sauces in small bowl; mix well.

tips cocktail sauce can be prepared 2 days ahead and refrigerated, covered

Prawns nestling on lettuce, served with lemon and the traditional sauce, makes a starter that remains a firm favourite. The quantity of prawns in our recipe can be reduced, if desired, and crab and/or oysters can be used.

Cooking salt is coarser than table salt but not as large-grained as sea salt; it is sold packaged in bags, in most supermarkets.
You need a large (around 28cm x 38cm) baking dish in order to accommodate the fish in this recipe.

salt-baked whole ocean trout in cream sauce

preparation time 30 minutes ▪ cooking time 1 hour 10 minutes
▪ serves 6

3kg cooking salt

4 egg whites

2.4kg whole sea trout

1.5kg tiny new potatoes

3 whole unpeeled bulbs garlic, halved horizontally

¼ cup (60ml) olive oil

15 sprigs fresh thyme

350g watercress, trimmed

saffron cream sauce

¾ cup (180ml) dry white wine

¼ cup (60ml) white wine vinegar

1 tablespoon lemon juice

pinch saffron threads

½ cup (125ml) cream

170g butter, chilled, chopped finely

1 Preheat oven to moderately hot.

2 Mix salt with egg whites in medium bowl (mixture will have the consistency of wet sand). Spread about half of the salt mixture evenly over the base of a large baking dish; place fish on salt mixture then cover completely (except for tail) with remaining salt mixture. Bake in moderately hot oven 1 hour.

3 Meanwhile, combine potatoes, garlic, oil and thyme in large shallow baking dish; place in oven on shelf below fish. Bake, uncovered, in moderately hot oven about 50 minutes or until potatoes are tender.

4 Make saffron cream sauce.

5 Remove fish from oven; break salt crust with heavy knife, taking care not to cut into fish. Discard salt crust; transfer fish to large serving plate. Carefully remove skin from fish; flake meat into large pieces.

6 Divide watercress, potatoes and garlic among serving plates; top with fish, drizzle sauce over fish.

▪ saffron cream sauce Combine wine, vinegar, juice and saffron in medium saucepan; bring to a boil. Boil until mixture is reduced to about a third. Add cream; return to boil, then whisk in butter, one piece at a time, until mixture thickens slightly. Pour into medium jug; cover to keep warm.

salmon fishcakes

preparation time 20 minutes (plus refrigeration time)
■ cooking time 15 minutes ■ makes 8

5 small potatoes (480g)

440g can salmon

1 trimmed stick celery (75g),
chopped finely

1 small white onion (80g), grated

1 small red pepper (150g),
chopped finely

1 tablespoon finely chopped fresh
flat-leaf parsley

1 teaspoon grated lemon rind

1 tablespoon lemon juice

½ cup (75g) plain flour, approx.

1 egg, beaten lightly

2 tablespoons milk

1 cup (100g) packaged
breadcrumbs, approx.

1 cup (70g) stale breadcrumbs,
approx.

vegetable oil, for deep frying

1 Boil, steam or microwave potatoes until tender; drain well. Place in medium bowl; mash using fork or potato masher until smooth. Drain salmon well; remove skin and bones. Add to bowl; mash using fork. Add celery, onion, pepper, parsley, rind and juice; mix well using fork. Cover; refrigerate 30 minutes.

2 Divide salmon mixture evenly into eight portions; shape each portion into patty; dust with flour. Shake off excess flour; brush fishcake with combined egg and milk. Toss in combined breadcrumbs; reshape if necessary.

3 Place fishcakes into frying basket, in batches. Lower gently into hot oil; deep-fry about 2 minutes or until golden. Drain on kitchen paper. Serve with lemon wedges, if desired.

tips fishcakes can be prepared a day ahead and refrigerated, covered ■ to reheat, place 1cm apart on a flat oven tray; cover with foil, then slash holes in the foil to allow steam to escape; bake in moderate oven for about 15 minutes or until hot ■ you can use any type of salmon, but must be drained well ■ tuna can be used instead of salmon, if you prefer ■ do not add any butter, milk, cream or water to the mashed potato – moisture will make the fishcakes too soft

fish fingers with potato and pea mash

preparation time 35 minutes ▪ cooking time 20 minutes
▪ serves 4

1kg white fish fillets, skinned,
chopped coarsely
2 tablespoons coarsely chopped
fresh chives
1 teaspoon curry powder
½ cup (75g) plain flour
2 eggs, beaten lightly
2 tablespoons milk
⅔ cup (70g) packaged
breadcrumbs
⅔ cup (60g) desiccated coconut
vegetable oil, for shallow-frying

potato and pea mash
1kg potatoes, chopped coarsely
1 cup (125g) frozen peas
40g butter
½ cup (125ml) milk

1 Grease 19cm x 29cm baking tin.
2 Process fish fillets, chives and curry powder, pulsing, until mixture forms a smooth paste. Using spatula, press this mixture evenly into prepared tin; turn out onto tray lined with baking-parchment. Cut mixture into eight 19cm slices; cut each slice in half to make 16 fingers.
3 Pat fish fingers with flour, shaking away excess carefully; dip into combined egg and milk then in combined breadcrumbs and coconut.
4 Heat oil in large frying pan; shallow-fry fish fingers, in batches, until browned lightly and cooked through. Drain on absorbent paper.
5 Meanwhile, make potato and pea mash. Serve with fish fingers.

▪ potato and pea mash Boil, steam or microwave potato and peas, separately, until tender; drain. Mash potato in large bowl with butter and milk until smooth. Mash peas in small bowl until crushed. Add peas to potato mash; using wooden spoon, gently marble peas through potato.

creamy fish pies

preparation time 25 minutes ▪ cooking time 35 minutes
▪ serves 4

2½ cups (625ml) milk

½ small brown onion (40g)

1 bay leaf

6 black peppercorns

4 x 170g white fish fillets, skinned

3 large potatoes (900g), chopped
coarsely

600g celeriac, chopped coarsely

1 egg yolk

½ cup (40g) finely grated parmesan

¾ cup (180ml) cream

60g butter

¼ cup (35g) plain flour

2 tablespoons coarsely chopped fresh
flat-leaf parsley

1 Place milk, onion, bay leaf and peppercorns in large saucepan; bring to a boil. Add fish, reduce heat; simmer, covered, about 5 minutes or until cooked through. Remove fish from pan; divide fish among four 1½-cup (375ml) ovenproof dishes. Strain milk through sieve into medium jug. Discard solids; reserve milk.

2 Boil, steam or microwave potato and celeriac, separately, until tender; drain. Push potato and celeriac through sieve into large bowl; stir in yolk, cheese, ¼ cup of the cream and half of the butter until smooth. Cover to keep warm.

3 Meanwhile, melt remaining butter in medium saucepan; add flour, cook, stirring, about 3 minutes or until mixture bubbles and thickens slightly. Gradually stir in reserved milk and remaining cream; cook, stirring, until mixture boils and thickens. Stir in parsley.

4 Divide sauce among dishes; cover each with potato mixture. Place pies on oven tray; place under hot grill until browned lightly.

meat & poultry

beef and onion casserole

preparation time 20 minutes ▯ cooking time 1 hour 30 minutes
▯ serves 4

1kg beef chuck steak, cut into 2cm dice
⅓ cup (50g) plain flour
2 tablespoons olive oil
2 small brown onions (200g),
chopped coarsely
2 cloves garlic, crushed
150g mushrooms, quartered
1 cup (250ml) dry red wine
400g can crushed tomatoes
2 cups (500ml) beef stock
2 tablespoons tomato paste

1 Coat beef in flour, shake away excess. Heat half the oil in large
saucepan; cook beef, in batches, until browned all over. Heat
remaining oil in same pan; cook onion, garlic and mushrooms,
stirring, until onion softens.
2 Return beef to pan with wine, undrained tomatoes, stock and
paste; bring to a boil. Reduce heat; simmer, covered, 40 minutes.
Uncover; simmer about 40 minutes or until meat is tender and
sauce thickens slightly, stirring occasionally.

If beef does not release enough excess oil during cooking, you may have to use melted butter in the patty-pan holes when making yorkshire puddings.

roast beef with yorkshire puddings

preparation time 40 minutes (plus refrigeration time) ▪ cooking time 1 hour 45 minutes ▪ serves 8

2kg corner piece beef topside roast

2 cups (500ml) dry red wine

2 bay leaves

6 black peppercorns

¼ cup (70g) wholegrain mustard

4 cloves garlic, sliced

4 sprigs fresh thyme

1 medium brown onion (150g), chopped coarsely

2 medium carrots (240g), chopped coarsely

1 large leek (500g), chopped coarsely

2 trimmed sticks celery (150g), chopped coarsely

1 tablespoon olive oil

2 tablespoons plain flour

1½ cups (375ml) beef stock

yorkshire puddings

1 cup (150g) plain flour

½ teaspoon salt

2 eggs, beaten lightly

½ cup (125ml) milk

½ cup (125ml) water

1 Combine beef, wine, bay leaves, peppercorns, mustard, garlic, thyme and onion in large bowl, cover; refrigerate 3 hours or overnight.

2 Preheat oven to moderate. Drain beef; reserve 1 cup (250ml) of the marinade.

3 Combine carrot, leek and celery in large roasting tin, place beef on top of vegetables; brush beef with oil. Bake, uncovered, in moderate oven about 1½ hours or until beef is browned and cooked as desired.

4 Remove beef from tin, wrap in foil; stand 20 minutes before serving.

5 Meanwhile, remove and discard vegetables with slotted spoon. Pour pan juices into jug, stand 5 minutes then pour off excess oil; reserve 1½ tablespoons of the oil for yorkshire puddings and 2 tablespoons of pan juices for gravy.

6 Heat reserved pan juices for gravy in same roasting tin, add flour; cook, stirring, until bubbling. Gradually add reserved marinade and stock; cook, stirring, until mixture boils and thickens.

7 Strain gravy into heatproof jug. Serve beef with gravy and yorkshire puddings.

▪ **yorkshire puddings** Sift flour and salt into medium bowl, make well in centre; add combined egg, milk and water all at once. Using wooden spoon, gradually stir in flour from side of bowl until batter is smooth. Cover; allow to stand 30 minutes. Divide the reserved oil among 12-hole (2 tablespoon/40ml) patty tin; heat in hot oven 2 minutes. Divide batter among holes; bake about 15 minutes or until puddings are golden.

beef and vegetables in beer

preparation time 15 minutes ▪ cooking time 1 hour 45 minutes ▪ serves 6

1½ tablespoons vegetable oil

1.5kg boned and rolled beef brisket joint

2 large carrots (360g), chopped coarsely

2 large parsnips (360g), chopped coarsely

6 baby onions (150g)

6 baby new potatoes (240g)

2 x 375ml cans beer

1 Heat oil in large roasting tin; cook beef until browned. Remove from dish.

2 Add vegetables to tin; cook, stirring, until browned all over. Return beef to tin; add beer. Cook, covered, in moderately hot oven 45 minutes.

3 Remove vegetables to flat oven tray. Cover loosely with foil; return to oven.

4 Turn beef; cook, uncovered, about 30 minutes or until beef is cooked through. Remove beef from tin; wrap in foil.

5 Place roasting tin over heat; simmer, uncovered, until liquid reduces to about 1 cup (250ml). Serve sliced beef with vegetables and sauce.

oxtail stew

preparation time 25 minutes ▪ cooking time 2 hours ▪ serves 6

2kg coarsely chopped oxtail

plain flour

60g butter or lard

2 large brown onions (400g), sliced thinly

2 cloves garlic, crushed

2 teaspoons coarsely chopped fresh rosemary

¼ cup (60ml) dry red wine

2 large parsnips (360g), sliced thickly

2 medium carrots (240g), sliced thickly

3 cups (750ml) beef stock

1 teaspoon freshly ground black pepper

2 medium courgettes (240g), sliced thickly

1 cup (250ml) tomato puree

1 tablespoon coarsely chopped fresh parsley

1 Toss oxtail in flour; shake away excess flour. Heat butter in large saucepan; cook oxtail, in batches, stirring, until browned well all over. Drain on absorbent kitchen paper.

2 Add onion, garlic and rosemary to pan; cook, stirring, until onion is soft. Add wine; cook, stirring, until liquid reduces by half.

4 Return oxtail to pan; add parsnip, carrot, stock and pepper. Cook, covered, 1¼ hours.

5 Add courgettes, puree and parsley; cook, uncovered, 20 minutes or until oxtail is tender.

tips best made a day ahead and refrigerated, covered ▪ suitable for freezing

Good, old-fashioned rissoles
are both tasty and wholesome.
Use good-quality mince, or
process your own steak; rump
steak is ideal.

rissoles with mushroom sauce

preparation time 15 minutes ▪ cooking time 25 minutes
▪ makes 4

375g minced beef

1 small brown onion (80g), chopped finely

1 small carrot (70g), grated coarsely

1 small red pepper (150g), chopped finely

½ teaspoon dried thyme

1 clove garlic, crushed

1 egg, beaten lightly

¼ cup (35g) plain flour, approx.

15g butter

2 teaspoons vegetable oil

mushroom sauce

2 tablespoons plain flour

2 tablespoons dry red wine

1 cup (250ml) beef stock

3 green onions, chopped finely

60g button mushrooms, sliced thinly

1 Combine mince, onion, carrot, pepper, thyme, garlic and egg in medium bowl. Mix using wooden spoon until ingredients are well combined.

2 Divide mixture into four equal portions. Roll into balls; flatten slightly into rissole shapes. Place flour in shallow bowl or plate. Toss rissoles in flour; shake off excess flour.

3 Heat butter and oil in medium frying pan over medium heat. Cook rissoles about 10 minutes on each side or until cooked through. Drain on absorbent paper.

▪ mushroom sauce Measure approximately 2 tablespoons of the pan drippings into small saucepan. Stir in flour; stir constantly over medium heat about 1 minute or until flour mixture browns lightly. Gradually stir in combined wine and stock; stir constantly over high heat until sauce boils and thickens. Add onion and mushrooms to sauce; simmer 2 minutes. Place rissoles on serving plates; pour sauce over rissoles and serve with the vegetables of your choice.

sausage casserole

800g thick beef sausages

20g butter

1 medium brown onion (150g),
chopped coarsely

1 tablespoon curry powder

2 teaspoons plain flour

2 large carrots (360g), chopped
coarsely

2 trimmed celery stalks (200g),
chopped coarsely

500g baby new potatoes, halved

2 cups (500ml) beef stock

1 cup loosely packed fresh
flat-leaf parsley leaves

preparation time 20 minutes cooking time 45 minutes
 serves 4

1 Cook sausages, in batches, in heated, deep, large frying pan
until cooked through. Cut each sausage into thirds.

2 Melt butter in same cleaned pan; cook onion, stirring, until soft.
Add curry powder and flour; cook, stirring, 2 minutes.

3 Add vegetables and stock; bring to a boil. Reduce heat;
simmer, covered, about 15 minutes or until vegetables are tender.
Add sausages; simmer, uncovered, until sauce thickens slightly.
Stir in parsley.

steak and kidney pie

preparation time 25 minutes ▪ cooking time 1 hour 30 minutes ▪ serves 6

300g beef ox kidneys

1.5g beef chuck steak, chopped coarsely

2 medium brown onions (300g), sliced thinly

1 cup (250ml) beef stock

1 tablespoon soy sauce

¼ cup (35g) plain flour

½ cup (125ml) water

2 sheets ready-rolled puff pastry

1 egg, beaten lightly

1 Remove fat from kidneys; chop kidneys finely. Combine kidneys, beef, onion, stock and sauce in large saucepan; simmer, covered, about 1 hour or until beef is tender.

2 Stir blended flour and water into beef mixture; stir until mixture boils and thickens. Transfer to 1.5 litre (6-cup) ovenproof dish.

3 Cut pastry into 6cm rounds. Overlap rounds on beef mixture; brush with egg. Cook in moderate oven about 15 minutes or until browned.

liver, mushroom and bacon pies

preparation time 15 minutes ▮ cooking time 30 minutes ▮ serves 4

500g lamb's liver

2 tablespoons olive oil

1 clove garlic, crushed

1 medium brown onion (150g), chopped finely

4 bacon rashers (280g), rind removed, chopped coarsely

200g button mushrooms, quartered

2 tablespoons plain flour

½ cup (125ml) dry red wine

1½ cups (375ml) beef stock

1 sheet ready-rolled butter puff pastry

1 egg yolk

1 tablespoon milk

1 Preheat oven to hot (220°C/200°C fan-assisted). Line oven tray with baking parchment.

2 Discard membrane and any fat from liver; chop coarsely. Heat half of the oil in large non-stick frying pan; cook liver, in batches, over high heat until browned and cooked as desired.

3 Heat remaining oil in same pan; cook garlic, onion, bacon and mushrooms, stirring, until onion softens. Add flour; cook, stirring, until mixture thickens and bubbles. Gradually add wine and stock; stir until mixture boils and thickens. Return liver to pan.

4 Cut four 9.5cm rounds from pastry sheet; place on prepared tray, brush with combined egg and milk. Bake, uncovered, in hot oven for about 5 minutes or until rounds are browned lightly.

5 Divide liver mixture among four 1¼-cup (310ml) ramekins; top with pastry rounds.

roast lamb with cauliflower cheese

preparation time 30 minutes ▪ cooking time 1 hour 10 minutes
▪ serves 6

2kg lamb leg
3 sprigs fresh rosemary, chopped
coarsely
½ teaspoon sweet paprika
1kg potatoes, chopped coarsely
500g piece pumpkin, chopped
coarsely
3 small brown onions (240g),
halved
2 tablespoons olive oil
2 tablespoons plain flour
1 cup (250ml) chicken stock
¼ cup (60ml) dry red wine

cauliflower cheese
1 small cauliflower (1kg),
broken into florets
50g butter
¼ cup (35g) plain flour
2 cups (500ml) milk
¾ cup (90g) coarsely grated
cheddar cheese

1 Preheat oven to moderately hot (200°C/180°C fan-assisted).
2 Place lamb in large lightly oiled roasting tin; using sharp knife, score
skin at 2cm intervals, sprinkle with rosemary and paprika. Roast lamb,
uncovered, in moderately hot oven for 15 minutes.
3 Reduce heat to moderate (180°C/160°C fan-assisted); roast lamb,
uncovered, about 45 minutes or until cooked as desired.
4 Meanwhile, place potato, pumpkin and onion, in single layer, in large
shallow baking dish; drizzle with oil. Roast, uncovered, in moderate oven
for last 45 minutes of lamb cooking time.
5 Make cauliflower cheese.
6 Remove lamb and vegetables from oven; cover to keep warm. Strain
pan juices from lamb into medium jug. Return ¼ cup of the pan juices
to flameproof dish over medium heat, add flour; cook, stirring, about
5 minutes or until mixture bubbles and browns. Gradually add stock and
wine; cook over high heat, stirring, until gravy boils and thickens.
7 Strain gravy; serve with sliced lamb, roasted vegetables and cauliflower
cheese.

▪ **cauliflower cheese** Boil, steam or microwave cauliflower until
tender; drain. Melt butter in medium saucepan, add flour; cook, stirring,
until mixture bubbles and thickens. Gradually add milk; cook, stirring, until
mixture boils and thickens. Stir in half of the cheese. Preheat grill. Place
cauliflower in 1.5-litre (6-cup) shallow flameproof dish; pour cheese sauce
over cauliflower, sprinkle with remaining cheese. Place under preheated grill
about 10 minutes or until browned lightly.

slow-roasted lamb shanks with caramelised red onion

preparation time 20 minutes ▪ cooking time 4 hours 30 minutes ▪ serves 4

1 tablespoon olive oil
8 trimmed lamb shanks (1.2kg)
1 tablespoon sugar
1½ cups (375ml) dry red wine
2 cups (500ml) beef stock
3 cloves garlic, crushed
20g butter
1 small brown onion (80g),
chopped finely
1 trimmed celery stick (75g),
chopped finely
1 tablespoon plain flour
1 tablespoon tomato paste
4 sprigs fresh rosemary, chopped
coarsely

caramelised onion
40g butter
2 medium red onions (340g),
sliced thinly
¼ cup (50g) brown sugar
¼ cup (60ml) balsamic vinegar

1 Preheat oven to low. Heat oil in large flameproof baking dish; cook lamb until browned all over. Stir in sugar, wine, stock and garlic; bring to a boil. Transfer lamb to slow oven; bake, covered, 4 hours, turning twice during cooking. Remove lamb from dish; cover to keep warm. Pour liquid from dish into large heatproof jug.
2 Return dish to heat, melt butter; cook onion and celery, stirring, until celery is just tender. Stir in flour; cook, stirring, 2 minutes. Add reserved liquid, tomato paste and rosemary; bring to a boil. Simmer, uncovered, stirring until mixture boils and thickens; strain wine sauce into large heatproof jug. Serve lamb with wine sauce and caramelised onion.

▪ caramelised onion Melt butter in medium saucepan; cook onion, stirring, about 15 minutes or until browned and soft. Stir in sugar and vinegar; cook, stirring, about 15 minutes or until onion is caramelised.

lancashire hot pot

preparation time 15 minutes ▪ cooking time 3 hours ▪ serves 4

8 lamb neck chops (1kg)
3 medium brown onions (450g), sliced thinly
3 large potatoes (900g), sliced thinly
4 bacon rashers (285g), chopped finely
1¾ cups (430ml) beef stock
30g butter, chopped coarsely

1 Trim fat from chops; place chops in 3 litre (12-cup) ovenproof casserole dish. Top with a layer of onion, potato and bacon. Repeat layering, ending with potatoes. Pour over stock; top with butter.

2 Cook, covered, in moderately slow oven 2 hours. Remove cover; cook about 1 hour or until chops are tender.

3 Serve with baby carrots, if desired.

irish stew

preparation time 15 minutes ▢ cooking time 1 hours 20 minutes ▢ serves 8

¼ cup (60ml) vegetable oil

2kg lamb neck chops

1 medium leek (350g), chopped finely

3 large potatoes (900g), chopped coarsely

2 medium carrots (240g), chopped coarsely

1 tablespoon finely chopped fresh thyme

1 litre (4 cups) lamb or chicken stock

1 Heat half of the oil in large pan; cook chops, in batches, until browned lightly all over. Remove from pan.

2 Heat remaining oil in pan; cook leek, stirring, until just tender.

3 Add potato, carrot and thyme, then return chops to pan with stock; simmer, covered, about 1 hour or until chops are tender.

tips suitable for freezing

roast pork with crackling and vegetables

preparation time 30 minutes ▪ cooking time 2 hours 10 minutes (plus standing time) ▪ serves 4

1.5kg boned loin of pork
1 tablespoon vegetable oil
2 teaspoons coarse cooking salt
4 large potatoes (1.2kg)
1 medium sweet potato (400g),
cut into pieces
1 tablespoon vegetable oil, extra
200g broccoli

apricot stuffing
⅓ cup (25g) stale breadcrumbs
¼ cup (35g) finely chopped
dried apricots
2 tablespoons finely chopped
walnuts or pecans
1 tablespoon coarsely chopped
fresh flat-leaf parsley
3 teaspoons sweet sherry

1 Unroll loin and make a cut in the fleshy part; this gives you a place to put the stuffing.
2 Turn loin over; score rind using sharp knife. Make sure you cut into the fat underneath rind; this will help rind to crisp and crackle during cooking.
3 Place apricot stuffing along flap; roll loin up firmly.
4 Tie loin firmly together using kitchen string.
5 Brush pork with oil; rub surface with salt. Place pork in roasting tin; bake in hot oven about 20 minutes or until rind of pork begins to crackle.
6 Meanwhile, peel and halve potatoes; place cut-side down on board. Using a sharp knife, cut potato halves into 5mm slices, but not cutting through base of potato. (These are called hasselback potatoes.)
7 Reduce oven temperature to moderate; add sweet potato and potato to baking dish. Brush vegetables with extra oil. Bake further 1 hour or until juices run clear when pork is pierced with skewer in meatiest part and vegetables are tender and browned. (Check vegetables after 45 minutes and, if already cooked, remove; keep warm.) An occasional basting or brushing with some of the pan drippings will be enough to brown the food.
8 Remove cooked pork from oven. Cover with foil; stand 10 minutes. Cut away string; slice pork thickly and place on heated serving plates. Serve with sweet potato, potatoes, boiled, steamed or microwaved broccoli and apple sauce (see page 56).

▪ apricot stuffing Combine breadcrumbs, apricots, nuts and parsley in medium bowl. Stir in sherry; mix well.

Apple sauce is the traditional accompaniment to roast pork. You can buy canned pie apple and blend or process it until smooth, then sweeten it to your taste with sugar or honey. Or buy apple prepared for babies or bottled apple sauce. However, it is quick and easy to make. We used a granny smith apple in this recipe.

rack of pork with apple sauce

preparation time 30 minutes ▪ cooking time 1 hour 30 minutes
▪ serves 6

coarse salt
1.3kg pork rack (6 cutlets)
1.25kg desiree potatoes, halved
750g pumpkin, chopped coarsely
1 tablespoon olive oil

apple sauce
1 small apple (130g)
1 tablespoon sugar
¼ cup (60ml) water
pinch ground cinnamon

1 Preheat oven to very hot. Rub salt evenly into rind of pork. Cover bones with foil to prevent burning. Place pork, rind-side up, in large baking dish; bake, uncovered, in very hot oven about 35 minutes or until rind is blistered and browned.
2 Place potatoes and pumpkin in separate baking dish, drizzle with oil. Reduce oven temperature to moderate; bake pork and vegetables, uncovered, about 40 minutes or until pork is cooked through. Remove pork from dish; cover with foil to keep warm.
3 Increase oven temperature to very hot; bake vegetables for 15 minutes or until browned and tender. Serve pork with vegetables and apple sauce.

▪ apple sauce Peel apple; cut into quarters. Remove core; slice apple. Combine apple, sugar, the water and cinnamon in medium saucepan; cover. Bring to a boil; reduce heat. Simmer, covered, about 5 minutes or until apple is pulpy. Whisk or stir until sauce is smooth. Serve hot or cold.

pork steaks with two sauces

preparation time 10 minutes ▪ cooking time 15 minutes
▪ serves 2

2 butterfly pork steaks (310g)
3 teaspoons olive oil

caraway sauce
1 teaspoon caraway seeds
2 teaspoons plain flour
½ cup (125ml) chicken stock
2 teaspoons tomato paste
1 tablespoon malt vinegar
1 teaspoon brown sugar

redcurrant jelly sauce
2 teaspoons plain flour
½ cup (125ml) chicken stock
1 tablespoon redcurrant jelly
1 tablespoon coarsely chopped
fresh chives

1 Use sharp knife to trim excess fat from pork. Heat oil in large frying pan; cook pork over high heat about 5 minutes on each side or until golden brown and tender. Remove pork from pan. Cover; keep warm in very slow oven while making sauce. Drain away pan drippings except for 2 teaspoons.
2 Serve with sauce and vegetables of your choice.

▪ **caraway sauce** Heat pan drippings in frying pan; cook seeds, covered, about 1 minute or until seeds begin to crack. Add flour; stir constantly over high heat about 1 minute or until mixture browns lightly. Remove pan from heat. Gradually stir in stock; stir until smooth. Stir in tomato paste, vinegar and sugar. Return pan to heat; stir constantly over high heat until mixture boils and thickens.

▪ **redcurrant jelly sauce** Heat pan drippings in frying pan; cook flour, stirring constantly over high heat until mixture browns lightly. Remove pan from heat. Gradually stir in stock; stir until smooth. Return pan to heat; stir constantly over high heat until mixture boils and thickens. Stir in jelly and chives. You can either leave small pieces of jelly suspended in the sauce, or continue to stir over heat until jelly is melted.

roast chicken and chips

preparation time 30 minutes ■ cooking time 1 hour 45 minutes
(plus standing time) ■ serves 4

1.5kg chicken
15g butter, melted

herb stuffing
1½ cups (105g) stale breadcrumbs
1 trimmed stick celery (75g), chopped finely
1 small white onion (80g), chopped finely
1 teaspoon dried mixed herbs
1 egg, beaten lightly

1   Remove and discard any fat from cavity of chicken.
2   Fill cavity of chicken with stuffing; do not pack in tightly as bread
expands during cooking and the stuffing will become a solid mass.
3   Place chicken on board, breast-side up. Secure chicken with
string by looping string around tail end; bring string around ends
of drumsticks. Turn chicken breast-side down and secure string
around wings.
4   Place chicken on rack over roasting tin. Half-fill tin with water;
it should not touch the chicken. Using small pastry brush, brush
chicken with butter; bake in moderately hot oven 15 minutes.
Reduce heat to moderate; bake 1½ hours.
5   Pierce skin and flesh of chicken in thickest part of drumstick;
the juices will be clear if chicken is cooked. Stand chicken
10 minutes before breaking or cutting into serving-sized pieces.
Serve with chips.

■ herb stuffing Using hand or wooden spoon, combine
breadcrumbs, celery, onion, herbs and egg in medium bowl;
mix well.

PERFECT CHIPS
4 large potatoes (1.2kg)
vegetable oil, for deep-frying

1   Peel potatoes; cut into even-
sized chips. Dry thoroughly with
tea-towel before frying.
2   Heat enough of the oil in deep
pan to come halfway up sides.
Add chips gradually so oil doesn't
spatter. Cook for a few minutes or
until they barely change colour;
drain well on absorbent paper.
3   Fry chips again until light
golden brown. Drain well on
kitchen paper; serve immediately.

tips the secret of making good
chips – crisp on the outside, soft
and fluffy in the middle – largely
depends on the type of potato
used. Generally, a hard, dry potato
gives good results ■ if making a
large quantity of chips, invest in a
deep-fat fryer ■ the double frying
method gives the best results; after
the first fry, the temperature of the
oil will drop; reheat the oil then fry
chips until done

chicken, leek and mushroom pies

preparation time 15 minutes ▮
cooking time 45 minutes ▮ serves 4

1 tablespoon vegetable oil
1 medium leek (350g), sliced thinly
2 rindless bacon rashers (130g), sliced thinly
200g mushrooms, halved
1 tablespoon plain flour
1 cup (250ml) chicken stock
⅓ cup (80ml) cream
1 tablespoon dijon mustard
3 cups (480g) coarsely chopped cooked chicken
1 sheet ready-rolled puff pastry, quartered

1 Preheat oven to 200°C/180°C fan-assisted.
2 Heat oil in medium saucepan; cook leek, bacon and mushrooms, stirring, until leek softens. Stir in flour; cook, stirring, until mixture thickens and bubbles. Gradually add stock; cook, stirring, until mixture boils and thickens. Stir in cream, mustard and chicken.
3 Divide mixture among four 1-cup (250ml) ovenproof dishes; top each with a pastry quarter. Bake, uncovered, in oven, about 20 minutes or until browned.

chicken and vegetable pasties

preparation time 15 minutes
cooking time 30 minutes ▪ serves 4

2 teaspoons vegetable oil
2 cloves garlic, crushed
1 medium brown onion (150g), chopped finely
1½ cups (240g) coarsely chopped leftover cooked chicken
2 cups (240g) frozen pea, corn and carrot mixture
2 teaspoons dijon mustard
½ cup (120g) sour cream
¼ cup (30g) coarsely grated cheddar cheese
4 sheets ready-rolled puff pastry
1 egg, beaten lightly

1 Preheat oven to 220°C/200°C fan-assisted. Lightly oil oven tray.
2 Heat oil in large frying pan; cook garlic and onion, stirring, until onion softens.
3 Add chicken, frozen vegetables, mustard, sour cream and cheese; stir until hot.
4 Cut one 22cm round from each pastry sheet. Place a quarter of the filling in centre of each round. Brush edge of pastry with egg; fold over to enclose filling, pinching edge together to seal.
5 Place pasties on tray; brush with remaining egg. Bake in oven about 30 minutes or until browned lightly.

chicken breasts with green peppercorn sauce

preparation time 5 minutes ▪ cooking time 20 minutes (plus standing time) ▪ serves 2

2 chicken breast fillets (340g)
30g butter
1 tablespoon plain flour
½ cup (125ml) chicken stock
2 teaspoons drained canned green peppercorns
1 tablespoon cream

1 Trim any excess fat from chicken. Melt butter in small frying pan; cook chicken over medium heat about 5 minutes each side or until tender and browned lightly. Remove chicken from pan; cover with foil to keep warm.

2 Sprinkle flour into frying pan; stir constantly over high heat until mixture is browned lightly.

3 Remove from heat; gradually stir in stock. Return to heat; stir constantly over high heat until sauce boils and thickens.

4 Add peppercorns and cream to sauce; stir over high heat, without boiling, until sauce is heated through. Serve immediately over chicken.

tips canned green peppercorns are available from supermarkets and delicatessens

turkey steaks with mustard cream sauce on bacon mash

preparation time 15 minutes ■ cooking time 30 minutes ■ serves 4

20g butter
8 turkey steaks (880g)
2 shallots (50g), chopped finely
1 clove garlic, crushed
½ cup (125ml) dry white wine
½ cup (125ml) cream
2 teaspoons wholegrain mustard

bacon mash

1kg potatoes, chopped coarsely
2 bacon rashers (140g), rind removed,
chopped coarsely
20g butter
¼ cup (60ml) cream
1 tablespoon coarsely chopped chives

1 Make bacon mash.
2 Melt half of the butter in large frying pan; cook steaks, in batches, until browned both sides.
3 Melt remaining butter in same pan; cook shallot and garlic, stirring, until soft. Add wine; bring to a boil. Reduce heat; simmer, uncovered, about 5 minutes or until almost evaporated. Stir in cream and mustard then return steaks to pan; bring to a boil. Reduce heat; simmer, covered, about 10 minutes or until steaks are cooked through.
4 Serve with chive and bacon mash, drizzled with sauce.

■ **bacon mash** Boil, steam or microwave potato until tender; drain. Cook bacon in small frying pan; drain on kitchen paper. Mash potato in large bowl with butter and cream until smooth. Stir in bacon and chives.

tips try using a dijon mustard with green peppercorns instead of wholegrain the next time you make this recipe – with the wine and the cream, it's a match made in culinary heaven.

slow-roasted turkey with port gravy

preparation time 30 minutes ▓ cooking time 6 hours
▓ serves 8

4kg turkey

¼ cup (60ml) chicken stock

½ cup (125ml) port

2 tablespoons brown sugar

2 tablespoons vegetable oil

2 tablespoons plain flour

sausagemeat stuffing

2 tablespoons vegetable oil

2 medium brown onions (300g), sliced

500g sausagemeat

4 cups (280g) stale breadcrumbs

2 tablespoons chopped fresh sage

½ cup (60g) chopped walnuts

1 Preheat oven to low. Discard neck and giblets from turkey. Rinse turkey under cold water; pat dry inside and out, tuck wings under body. Spoon seasoning loosely into cavity. Tie legs together with kitchen string.

2 Place turkey into oiled flameproof baking dish; pour stock and half of the port into dish. Cover baking dish tightly with greased foil (if thin, use two layers); bake in slow oven for 5½ hours. Remove foil, brush turkey with combined remaining port and sugar. Increase temperature to moderate; bake, uncovered, 30 minutes or until browned.

3 Remove turkey from dish; cover with foil to keep warm. Strain juices from dish into jug; remove fat from juices. You will need 3 cups (750ml) pan juices. Heat oil in same baking dish, stir in flour; stir over heat until well browned. Remove from heat, gradually stir in reserved pan juices; stir over heat until gravy boils and thickens, strain.

4 Serve turkey with gravy.

▓ **sausagemeat stuffing** Heat oil in large frying pan, add onion; cook, stirring, until browned, cool. Transfer onion to medium bowl; stir in remaining ingredients.

tips stuffing for your turkey can be made a day ahead; refrigerate separately ▓ fill turkey with stuffing close to cooking ▓ to keep leftover turkey, remove stuffing from cavity and refrigerate separately

straight to the sauce

A good sauce can turn a plain roast into something sublime. These recipes will ensure your roasts are unforgettable.

devilled sauce

makes 2 cups (500ml)

1 tablespoon olive oil
1 medium brown onion (150g), chopped finely
2 cloves garlic, crushed
1 teaspoon hot paprika
¼ cup (50g) firmly packed brown sugar
⅓ cup (80ml) cider vinegar
1 teaspoon Tabasco sauce
1 tablespoon worcestershire sauce
2 cups (500ml) beef stock
1 tablespoon cornflour
1 tablespoon water

1 Heat oil in medium frying pan, add onion and garlic; cook, stirring, until onion is soft. Stir in paprika, sugar and vinegar; cook, stirring, without boiling, until sugar dissolves.
2 Add sauces and stock; simmer, uncovered, about 15 minutes or until reduced to 2 cups. Stir in blended cornflour and water; stir until sauce boils and thickens.

gravy

makes 2 cups (500ml)

1 small brown onion (80g), chopped finely
2 tablespoons plain flour
½ cup (125ml) dry red wine
1½ cups (375ml) chicken or beef stock

1 Remove roast from roasting tin, cover to keep warm. Reserve 2 tablespoons of juices in roasting tin; discard remaining juice.
2 Add onion to tin; cook, stirring, until soft. Stir in flour; cook, stirring, about 5 minutes or until browned.
3 Pour in wine and stock; cook over high heat, stirring, until gravy boils and thickens. Strain gravy before serving.

mint sauce

makes 1¼ cups (310ml)

1 cup (250ml) cider vinegar
¼ cup (60ml) boiling water
¼ cup finely chopped fresh mint leaves
1 tablespoon brown sugar
1 teaspoon salt
¼ teaspoon ground black pepper

Combine ingredients in small bowl; stand
30 minutes before serving.

tips to adapt gravy into peppercorn or mushroom
gravy, place strained gravy in small saucepan, add
1 tablespoon drained canned green peppercorns or
100g finely sliced cooked button mushrooms and cook,
stirring, 2 minutes   for apple sauce, the traditional
accompaniment to roast pork, see page 56

vegetarian &
side dishes

caramelised leek tarts

preparation time 30 minutes ▦ cooking time 50 minutes
▦ serves 4

2 tablespoons olive oil

2 medium onions (300g), sliced thinly

2 medium leeks (700g), trimmed,
sliced thinly

1 tablespoon fresh thyme leaves

2 cups (400g) ricotta cheese

⅓ cup (25g) coarsely grated parmesan

1 egg, separated

4 sheets ready-rolled shortcrust pastry

1 Heat oil in large frying pan; cook onion and leek, stirring, about
15 minutes or until mixture starts to caramelise. Stir in thyme; cool.
2 Meanwhile, combine ricotta cheese, parmesan and egg yolk in
small bowl.
3 Preheat oven to 200°C/180°C fan-assisted. Oil two oven trays;
line with baking parchment.
4 Using 20cm plate as a guide, cut 1 round from each pastry
sheet; place two rounds on each tray. Divide cheese mixture
among rounds, leaving 4cm border around edges.
5 Divide leek mixture over rounds. Turn border of each tart up
around filling; brush upturned edges with egg white. Bake about
35 minutes or until pastry is browned lightly.

spinach and corn pasties

preparation time 20 minutes
cooking time 45 minutes ▪ serves 6

1 tablespoon vegetable oil
2 medium potatoes (400g), diced into 1cm pieces
1 small brown onion (80g), chopped finely
250g frozen spinach, thawed, drained
2 x 310g cans creamed corn
3 sheets ready-rolled shortcrust pastry
2 tablespoons milk

1 Heat half the oil in large frying pan; cook potato, stirring, until browned lightly. Add onion; cook, stirring, until soft. Combine potato, onion, spinach and corn in large bowl.
2 Preheat oven to 200°C/180°C fan-assisted.
3 Oil two baking trays. Cut pastry sheets in half diagonally. Divide filling among triangles, placing on one side; fold pastry in half to enclose filling, pressing edges with fork to seal.
4 Place pasties on trays; brush with milk. Bake about 30 minutes or until browned lightly.

barley and vegetable hotpot

preparation time 25 minutes ▪ cooking time
1 hour 5 minutes ▪ serves 6

1 cup (200g) pearl barley
1 tablespoon olive oil
2 medium brown onions (300g), chopped finely
2 medium carrots (350g), chopped coarsely
2 trimmed sticks celery (150g), chopped coarsely
2 cloves garlic, crushed
2 corn cobs (500g)
2 large parsnips (360g), chopped coarsely
2 cups (500ml) vegetable stock
1 cup (250ml) water
500g pumpkin, chopped coarsely
½ cup finely chopped flat-leaf parsley
2½ tablespoons miso paste

1 Place barley in large saucepan. Cover with water; bring to a boil. Reduce heat to low; cook, uncovered, 30 minutes or until tender. Drain; reserve.

2 Heat oil in large saucepan; cook onion, carrot, celery and garlic over medium heat, stirring occasionally, about 10 minutes or until vegetables are almost tender.

3 Remove corn kernels from cobs. Add corn kernels, parsnip, stock and the water to pan; cook, uncovered, over medium heat for 15 minutes
or until almost tender. Add pumpkin; cook further 5 minutes or until all vegetables are tender.

4 Stir in barley and parsley; cook until heated through.

5 Stir 1 teaspoon of miso into each cup of heated hotpot.

An old British favourite is given a new vegetarian Mediterranean twist in this recipe.

lentil cottage pie

preparation time 20 minutes ▪ cooking time 1 hour 15 minutes
▪ serves 4

4 medium potatoes (800g), chopped coarsely

½ cup (125ml) milk, warmed

4 spring onions, chopped finely

½ cup (100g) french green lentils

1 tablespoon olive oil

1 large brown onion (200g), chopped finely

1 medium red pepper (200g), chopped coarsely

2 medium courgettes (240g), chopped coarsely

1 medium aubergine (300g), chopped coarsely

2 cloves garlic, crushed

410g can crushed tomatoes

1 Boil, steam or microwave potato until tender; drain. Mash potato in large bowl with milk and spring onion until smooth.

2 Meanwhile, cook lentils in small saucepan of boiling water until just tender; drain. Rinse; drain.

3 Preheat oven to 200°C/180°C fan-assisted.

4 Heat oil in medium saucepan; cook brown onion, pepper, courgettes, aubergine and garlic, stirring, until vegetables soften. Add lentils and undrained tomato; bring to a boil. Reduce heat; simmer, about 10 minutes or until mixture has thickened.

5 Spoon mixture into lightly oiled shallow 2.5 litre (10-cup) baking dish; spread with potato. Bake, uncovered, in oven about 30 minutes or until top browns lightly.

scalloped potatoes

preparation time 20 minutes ▪ cooking time 1 hour 15 minutes ▪ serves 4

4 large old potatoes (1.2kg), peeled, sliced thinly
pinch ground nutmeg
1 cup (250ml) cream
¼ cup (20g) grated parmesan cheese
20g butter, chopped coarsely

1 Grease deep 19cm square cake pan; layer potatoes in pan. Sprinkle with nutmeg; pour over cream. Sprinkle with cheese; dot with butter.
2 Bake, covered, in moderate oven 30 minutes. Uncover; bake further 45 minutes or until top is browned and potatoes are tender.

tips do not use thickened cream in this recipe ▪ can be made 1 day ahead and refrigerated, covered

mushroom and broccoli baked spuds

preparation time 20 minutes
cooking time 1 hour 20 minutes   serves 4

5 large potatoes (1.2kg)
2 teaspoons vegetable oil
100g button mushrooms, sliced thinly
85g finely chopped broccoli florets
20g butter
2 tablespoons plain flour
1 cup (250ml) milk
½ cup (60g) coarsely grated cheddar cheese

1   Scrub potatoes; pierce skin. Place on greased oven tray; bake, uncovered, in moderate oven about 1 hour or until tender. When cool enough to handle, cut 1cm slice off one long side of each potato; scoop out potato flesh, leaving a 5mm shell. Reserve flesh; place shells on oven tray.
2   Heat oil in small saucepan; cook mushrooms and broccoli, stirring, until broccoli is just tender.
3   Heat butter in small saucepan; cook flour, stirring, until mixture is grainy. Remove from heat; gradually stir in milk. Stir over medium heat until sauce boils and thickens. Remove from heat; stir in half of the cheese.
4   Combine potato flesh, mushroom mixture and sauce in large bowl; mix well. Divide potato mixture among potato shells.
5   Sprinkle potatoes with remaining cheese. Bake, uncovered, in moderate oven about 10 minutes or until hot.

tips combine potato flesh with one finely chopped spring onion and 2 tablespoons each of sour cream and sweet chilli sauce. Divide filling among potato shells and serve topped with extra spring onion, sour cream and sweet chilli sauce

cheesy crushed roast potato and thyme

preparation time 15 minutes ▪ cooking time 30 minutes
▪ serves 4 as a side dish

50g butter
1 medium brown onion (150g),
sliced thinly
600g roast potatoes, halved
2 tablespoons plain flour
1 cup (250ml) milk
2 teaspoons finely chopped
fresh thyme
1 cup (120g) coarsely grated
cheddar

1 Preheat oven to 220°C/200°C fan-assisted. Oil four 1-cup (250ml) shallow ovenproof baking dishes.

2 Melt 10g of the butter in medium saucepan; cook onion, stirring, until softened.

3 Meanwhile, use potato masher to gently crush potato in large bowl; stir in onion mixture.

4 Melt remaining butter in same pan, add flour; cook, stirring, until mixture thickens and bubbles. Gradually stir in milk; cook, stirring, until white sauce boils and thickens. Remove from heat; stir in thyme and half the cheese.

5 Stir white sauce into potato mixture. Spoon mixture into dishes; sprinkle each with remaining cheese. Bake in oven about 20 minutes or until browned lightly.

parsnip purée

preparation time 15 minutes
cooking time 20 minutes   serves 6

6 large parsnips (1kg), chopped finely
1 teaspoon seasoned pepper
40g butter
2 tablespoons cream
1 tablespoon finely chopped fresh parsley

Boil, steam or microwave parsnips until tender;
drain. Blend or process parsnips with remaining
ingredients until smooth.

roasted sweet
potato purée

preparation time 15 minutes
cooking time 50 minutes   serves 4

1 large sweet potato (550g)
⅔ cup (160ml) thickened cream
¼ teaspoon ground cumin
¼ teaspoon mixed spice

Cut sweet potato into 4cm chunks; place onto
oven tray. Cover; bake in moderately hot oven
about 50 minutes or until tender. Blend or
process sweet potato with remaining ingredients
until smooth.

basic mashed potato

preparation time 15 minutes
cooking time 20 minutes   serves 4

4 medium old potatoes (800g)
40g butter
¼ cup (60ml) milk
1 teaspoon brown sugar

Peel potatoes; cut each into four even pieces.
Boil, steam or microwave potatoes until tender;
drain. Mash well using potato masher or fork, or
push potato through sieve. Add butter, milk and
sugar, beat until butter melts.

mashed potato variations

PINE NUT
Add ⅓ cup (50g) toasted pine nuts and 2 teaspoons finely chopped fresh rosemary to basic mashed potato; mix well.

LEEK & THYME
Heat 1 tablespoon vegetable oil in large saucepan; add 1 small, thinly sliced leek, 1 crushed clove garlic and 1 tablespoon finely chopped fresh thyme, and cook stirring, until leek is soft. Add 2 tablespoons dry white wine; cook, stirring, until wine evaporates. Stir leek mixture into basic mashed potato.

BACON & MUSTARD
Cook 4 finely chopped bacon rashers in large frying pan until crisp; drain on kitchen paper. Add bacon, 3 teaspoons wholegrain mustard and 1 tablespoon finely chopped fresh parsley to basic mashed potato; mix well.

puddings
& desserts

apple and blackberry jellies

preparation time 10 minutes (plus refrigeration time) ▦ serves 4

85g packet blackcurrant jelly
crystals
1 cup (150g) frozen blackberries
1 medium apple (150g), peeled,
cored, chopped finely
½ cup (125ml) whipping cream
1 tablespoon icing sugar

1 Prepare jelly according to packet instructions.
2 Divide blackberries and apple among four ¾-cup (180ml) glasses then pour jelly over the top. Refrigerate about 3 hours or until jelly has set.
3 Beat cream and icing sugar in small bowl with electric mixer until soft peaks form. Serve jellies topped with whipped cream.

traditional trifle

preparation time 25 minutes (plus refrigeration and standing time) ▪ cooking time 10 minutes ▪ serves 4

150g cake (bought or leftover sponge, butter or madeira cake)

2 tablespoons sweet sherry

85g packet raspberry jelly crystals

1 cup (250ml) boiling water

½ cup (125ml) cold water

425g can sliced peaches, drained

½ cup (125ml) whipping cream

2 teaspoons icing sugar

custard

1¾ cups (430ml) milk

¼ cup (30g) custard powder

2 tablespoons caster sugar

¼ cup (60ml) milk, extra

1 tablespoon sweet sherry

1 Cut cake into even-size pieces. Place in large serving dish; drizzle with sherry.

2 Combine jelly crystals and the boiling water in medium bowl; stir until jelly is dissolved. Stir in the cold water. Transfer mixture to medium jug; gently pour over back of spoon onto cake to prevent cake breaking up. Refrigerate until set.

3 Place peaches over jelly; top with custard. Refrigerate until set. Whip cream and icing sugar together until soft peaks form; use to decorate or spread over trifle. Add extra fruit, if desired.

▪ custard Place milk in medium saucepan. Bring to a boil; reduce heat. Blend custard powder and sugar with extra milk in small bowl; stir until smooth. Gradually stir into milk in saucepan; stir constantly over medium heat until mixture boils and thickens. Stir in sherry. Cover; stand 10 minutes.

berry trifle

preparation time 20 minutes (plus refrigeration time) ▇ cooking time 10 minutes ▇ serves 6

1 tablespoon custard powder
2 teaspoons caster sugar
1 cup milk
300ml whipping cream
2 teaspoons icing sugar
1 teaspoon vanilla extract
12 sponge-finger biscuits (180g)
1 cup (250ml) apple juice
300g frozen mixed berries

1 Combine custard powder with caster sugar and milk in small pan; stir over low heat until custard boils and thickens.
2 Beat cream, icing sugar and extract in small bowl with electric mixer until soft peaks form.
3 Dip biscuits, one at a time, in juice; cover base of 1.5-litre (6-cup) serving dish with some of the biscuits. Top with custard and half the berries. Top with remaining dipped biscuits, cream and berries. Refrigerate 2 hours.

Trifle is always a winner with all ages, and you can vary the ingredients to suit yourself or whatever you have on hand. For our traditional trifle, we used the method of setting the cake in jelly as a base, but some people prefer to place the cake in the bowl, sprinkle it with fruit juice or sherry, then add jelly and custard, nuts and fruit, according to the texture and flavour required.

lemon meringue pie

preparation time 30 minutes (plus refrigeration time)
▓ cooking time 35 minutes ▓ serves 10

½ cup (75g) cornflour
1 cup (220g) caster sugar
½ cup (125ml) lemon juice
1¼ cups (310ml) water
2 teaspoons finely grated
lemon rind
60g unsalted butter, chopped
3 eggs, separated
½ cup (110g) caster sugar, extra

pastry
1½ cups (225g) plain flour
1 tablespoon icing sugar
140g cold butter, chopped
1 egg yolk
2 tablespoons cold water

1 Make pastry.
2 Grease 24cm-round loose-based fluted flan tin. Roll pastry between sheets of baking parchment until large enough to line tin. Ease pastry into tin, press into base and side; trim edge. Cover; refrigerate 30 minutes.
3 Preheat oven to 240°C/220°C fan-assisted.
4 Place tin on oven tray. Line pastry case with baking parchment; fill with dried beans or rice. Bake 15 minutes; remove paper and beans carefully from pie shell. Bake about 10 minutes; cool pie shell, turn oven off.
5 Meanwhile, combine cornflour and sugar in medium saucepan; gradually stir in juice and the water until smooth. Cook, stirring, over high heat, until mixture boils and thickens. Reduce heat; simmer, stirring, 1 minute. Remove from heat; stir in rind, butter and egg yolks. Cool 10 minutes.
6 Spread filling into pie shell. Cover; refrigerate 2 hours.
7 Preheat oven to 240°C/220°C fan-assisted.
8 Beat egg whites in small bowl with electric mixer until soft peaks form; gradually add extra sugar, beating until sugar dissolves.
9 Roughen surface of filling with fork before spreading with meringue mixture. Bake about 2 minutes or until browned lightly.

▓ pastry Process flour, icing sugar and butter until crumbly. Add egg yolk and the water; process until ingredients come together. Knead dough on floured surface until smooth. Cover; refrigerate 30 minutes.

eton mess

preparation time 15 mins ▮ serves 6

500g strawberries, halved
1 tablespoon orange-flavoured liqueur
300ml whipping cream
2 tablespoons icing sugar
½ cup (140g) plain yogurt
10 mini meringue nests (100g), chopped coarsely

1 Combine strawberries and liqueur in medium bowl.
2 Beat cream and sugar in small bowl with electric mixer until soft peaks form. Fold in yogurt.
3 Place half of the strawberries in 1.25-litre (5-cup) serving dish. Top with half of the meringues and half of the cream mixture. Repeat layering with remaining strawberries, meringues and cream mixture.

lemon delicious pudding

preparation time 20 minutes ■
cooking time 45 minutes ■ serves 4

3 eggs
½ cup (110g) caster sugar
1 cup (250ml) milk
1 tablespoon self-raising flour
½ cup (125ml) lemon juice

1 Separate eggs; place whites and yolks in two separate small bowls. Add sugar to egg yolks in small bowl; beat using electric mixer until thick and creamy. Gradually beat in milk on low speed, then flour and lemon juice. Pour into large bowl.

2 Beat egg whites in small bowl using electric mixer until soft peaks form. Using a plastic spatula, fold into egg yolk mixture in two batches. Do not stir or beat, as you will deflate the mixture. The mixture will look a bit curdled at this stage.

3 Pour mixture into deep 1-litre (4-cup) ovenproof dish. Place dish in baking dish; add enough boiling water to baking dish to come halfway up side of ovenproof dish. Bake in moderate oven about 45 minutes or until firm to touch. Sprinkle with a little icing sugar, if desired.

tips lemon delicious should be served immediately

Bread and butter pudding is an old English favourite, originally devised to use up stale bread. The bread needs to be a little dry for best results. Use the jam and dried fruit of your choice. If the dried fruit is hard, chop and then soak in a little boiling water about 30 minutes or until soft; drain well before using.

bread and butter pudding

preparation time 15 minutes (plus standing time)
cooking time 44 minutes ▪ serves 4

3 eggs

2 tablespoons caster sugar

1 teaspoon vanilla essence

2½ cups (625ml) milk

30g butter

⅓ cup (110g) apricot jam

8 slices stale white bread

½ cup (75g) coarsely chopped dried apricots

¼ teaspoon ground cinnamon or nutmeg

1 Whisk eggs, sugar and essence together in medium bowl; whisk in milk gradually.

2 Spread butter and jam on each slice of bread; trim away crusts. Cut bread into halves or finger-length pieces. Place layer of bread in 3-cup (750ml) ovenproof dish. Add apricot and half of the custard mixture; stand 10 minutes to allow bread to soften.

3 Place remaining bread, buttered-side down, in dish; add remaining custard. Sprinkle lightly with cinnamon or nutmeg.

4 Place dish in baking dish; add enough boiling water to come halfway up sides of baking dish. Bake in moderate oven about 40 minutes or until just set.

tips custard can be made 3 days ahead and refrigerated, covered ▪ the pudding will not reheat successfully but is delicious served cold with cream or added fruit

baked egg custard

preparation time 5 minutes ▮ cooking time 45 minutes ▮ serves 6

6 eggs

1 teaspoon vanilla extract

⅓ cup (75g) caster sugar

1 litre (4 cups) hot milk

¼ teaspoon ground nutmeg

1 Preheat oven to 160°C/140°C fan-assisted. Grease shallow 1.5-litre (6-cup) ovenproof dish.

2 Whisk eggs, extract and sugar in large bowl; gradually whisk in hot milk. Pour custard mixture into dish; sprinkle with nutmeg.

3 Place dish in larger baking dish; add enough boiling water to come halfway up sides of dish. Bake, uncovered, about 45 minutes. Remove custard from large dish; stand 5 minutes before serving.

VARIATIONS

▮ **citrus** Stir ½ teaspoon each of finely grated orange, lime and lemon rind into hot milk mixture; omit nutmeg.

▮ **chocolate** Whisk ⅓ cup cocoa powder and ⅓ cup dark chocolate chips with eggs, extract and sugar; omit nutmeg.

▮ **coconut and cardamom** Omit hot milk; bring 2⅓ cups milk, 400ml can coconut milk, 3 bruised cardamom pods and 5cm strip lime rind to a boil. Remove from heat, stand 10 minutes. Strain; discard solids. Whisk milk mixture into egg mixture.

rice pudding

preparation time 15 minutes (plus standing time)
■ cooking time 1 hour 10 minutes ■ serves 8

2 cups (500ml) skimmed milk

1 vanilla pod, halved lengthways

2 eggs

1 egg white

½ cup (110g) caster sugar

1½ cups (225g) cooked long grain rice

½ cup (125ml) single cream

1 Preheat oven to moderately slow. Grease shallow oval 1.5-litre (6 cup) ovenproof dish.

2 Combine milk and vanilla pod in medium saucepan; bring to a boil. Remove from heat; stand, covered, 5 minutes.

3 Meanwhile, whisk eggs, egg white and sugar in medium bowl. Gradually whisk hot milk mixture into egg mixture; discard vanilla pod.

4 Spread rice into prepared dish; pour egg mixture carefully over rice. Place dish in large baking dish; add enough boiling water to baking dish to come halfway up side of pudding dish.

5 Bake, uncovered, in moderately slow oven about 1 hour or until set. Serve warm with cream.

VARIATION
■ **citrus rice** Stir 1 teaspoon each of finely grated lime and lemon rind and 2 teaspoons of finely grated orange rind into milk mixture in stage 2.

tips you need to cook about ½ cup of rice for this recipe

pancakes with lemon and sugar

preparation time 10 minutes ▪ cooking time 10 minutes ▪ makes about 15

2 cups (300g) plain flour

4 eggs, beaten lightly

2 cups (500ml) milk, approximately

40g butter

¼ cup (60ml) lemon juice, approximately

2 tablespoons sugar, approximately

1 Place flour in medium bowl. Make well in centre; gradually whisk or stir in egg and enough of the milk to make a thin, smooth batter. Alternatively, combine flour, egg and milk in blender or processor; blend or process until mixture is combined and smooth.

2 Heat heavy-base frying pan over high heat a few minutes; pan should be very hot. Place about ½ teaspoon butter in pan; swirl around pan until greased all over. Pour about ¼ cup of the batter from jug into centre of pan; quickly tilt pan so that batter runs from centre around edge.

3 When pancake is browned lightly underneath, turn and brown other side. This can be done using spatula or egg slide, or pancake can be tossed and flipped over back into the pan; this takes a little practice.

4 Serve pancakes, as they are made, on warm plates; spread one side with a little of the butter. Drizzle with juice; sprinkle with sugar.

apple crumble

preparation time 15 minutes
cooking time 35 minutes ▨ serves 4

5 large apples (1kg)
¼ cup (55g) caster sugar
¼ cup (60ml) water

crumble topping
½ cup (75g) self-raising flour
¼ cup (35g) plain flour
½ cup (110g) firmly packed brown sugar
100g cold butter, chopped
1 teaspoon ground cinnamon

1 Preheat oven to 180°C/160°C fan-assisted.
Grease deep 1.5-litre (6-cup) baking dish.
2 Peel, core and quarter apples. Combine apple,
sugar and the water in large saucepan; cook
over low heat, covered, about 10 minutes.
Drain; discard liquid.
3 Meanwhile, make crumble topping.
4 Place apples in dish; sprinkle with crumble.
Bake about 25 minutes.

▨ **crumble topping** Blend or process
ingredients until combined.

VARIATIONS
▨ **nut crumble** Stir in ⅓ cup roasted slivered
almonds and ⅓ cup coarsely chopped roasted
hazelnuts to crumble mixture.
▨ **muesli crumble** Prepare half the amount of
basic crumble mixture; stir in 1 cup toasted muesli.

old-fashioned apple pie

preparation time 50 minutes (plus refrigeration time) ■ cooking time
45 minutes (plus cooling time) ■ serves 8

1 cup (150g) plain flour
½ cup (75g) self-raising flour
¼ cup (35g) cornflour
¼ cup (30g) custard powder
2 tablespoons caster sugar
125g butter, chopped coarsely
1 egg, separated
¼ cup (60ml) water,
approximately

lemony apple filling

7 large apples (1.4kg)
½ cup (125ml) water
2 tablespoons sugar
¼ teaspoon ground cinnamon
1 teaspoon grated lemon rind

1 Combine flours, custard powder and half of the sugar in large bowl; rub in butter using fingertips or process in food processor until ingredients are just combined.

2 Add enough of the combined egg yolk and the water to make a firm dough. This can also be done in food processor. Turn dough onto lightly floured surface; knead gently until smooth. Cut dough in half; wrap in cling film. Refrigerate 30 minutes.

3 Roll out half of the pastry between sheets of cling film or greaseproof paper until large enough to line deep 23cm pie plate.

4 Remove top piece of film from pastry. Use remaining film to help turn pastry into pie plate. Carefully press pastry into pie plate; do not stretch pastry. Remove remaining film. Trim edge of pastry using sharp knife; reserve scraps.

5 Spoon cold apple filling evenly into pastry case; brush edge of pastry with lightly beaten egg white. Roll out remaining pastry as before; cover filling with pastry. Press edges together firmly; trim with knife. Using fingers, pinch edges to make a frill.

6 Roll out pastry scraps and cut leaf shapes from pastry, if desired, marking veins on leaves with small knife; brush pastry with egg white. Place leaves in position; brush leaves with egg white. Sprinkle pie evenly with remaining sugar.

7 Bake in moderately hot oven 20 minutes. Reduce heat to moderate; bake 20 minutes or until pie is golden brown.

■ lemony apple filling Peel, core and quarter apples; cut each quarter in half lengthways. Place in large saucepan with the water; bring to a boil. Reduce heat; cover. Cook about 5 minutes or until apples are just tender. Transfer apples to large bowl; gently stir in sugar, cinnamon and lemon rind. Cool to room temperature.

cakes

butterfly cakes

preparation time 30 minutes ▪ baking time 20 minutes
▪ makes 24

125g butter, softened
1 teaspoon vanilla extract
⅔ cup (150g) caster sugar
3 eggs
1½ cups (225g) self-raising flour
¼ cup (60ml) milk
½ cup (160g) jam
300ml double cream

1 Line two deep 12-hole bun tins with paper cases.
2 Combine butter, extract, sugar, eggs, flour and milk in bowl of electric mixer; beat on low speed until ingredients are just combined. Increase speed to medium, beat about 3 minutes, or until mixture is smooth and changed to a paler colour.
3 Drop slightly rounded tablespoons of mixture into paper cases. Bake in moderate oven about 20 minutes. Turn cakes onto wire racks, turn top-side up to cool.
4 Using sharp pointed vegetable knife, cut circle from top of each cake; cut circle in half to make two 'wings'. Fill cavities with jam and whipped cream. Place wings in position on top of cakes; top with strawberry pieces and dust with a little sifted icing sugar, if desired.

Butterfly cakes are made by removing a small circle from the top of each cake, filling the cavity with jam and cream, then topping with the two halves of the circle to create 'wings'.

tips use two paper cake cases in each bun tin hole for added stability for butterfly cakes.

scones

preparation time 15 minutes ▫ baking time 15 minutes
▫ makes about 10

2 cups (300g) self-raising flour
2 teaspoons sugar
15g butter, chopped coarsely
1 cup (250ml) milk,
approximately

1 Place flour and sugar in medium bowl; rub in butter using fingertips.
2 Make well in centre of flour mixture; add most of the milk.
3 Using a knife, 'cut' the milk through the flour mixture to mix to a soft, sticky dough. Add remaining milk only if needed for correct consistency.
4 Turn dough from bowl onto lightly floured surface. (Don't use too much flour or the balance of ingredients will be upset.)
5 Knead dough lightly until smooth. Press dough out gently and evenly to approximately 2cm thickness.
6 Dip 5cm cutter into flour; cut as many rounds as you can from the piece of dough. Place scones side by side, just touching, in lightly greased 20cm sandwich tin. Gently knead remaining dough into round shape again, making it a little thicker than the first time; using floured cutter, cut rounds from dough. The scones from this second handling will not be quite as light as those from the first.
7 Brush tops of rounds with a little of the extra milk.
8 Bake in very hot oven about 15 minutes, or until tops are browned and scones sound hollow when tapped using fingertips.

Scones served hot from the oven with butter or jam and cream are delightful for morning or afternoon tea. Often, cooks are judged by their scones, but there is no mystery about making light, fluffy scones; you must make a soft, sticky dough and the dough should be kneaded quickly and lightly. The rest is up to the oven; it should be very hot to help the scones rise quickly.

rock cakes

preparation time 15 minutes ■ cooking time 15 minutes ■ makes 18

2 cups (300g) self-raising flour
¼ teaspoon ground cinnamon
⅓ cup (75g) caster sugar
90g butter, chopped
1 cup (160g) sultanas
1 egg, beaten lightly
½ cup (125ml) milk
1 tablespoon caster sugar, extra

1 Preheat oven to 200°C/180°C fan-assisted. Grease two baking trays.
2 Sift flour, cinnamon and sugar into medium bowl; rub in butter. Stir in sultanas, egg and milk. Do not over mix.
3 Drop rounded tablespoons of mixture about 5cm apart onto trays; sprinkle with extra sugar. Bake about 15 minutes; cool on trays.

tips rock cakes can be stored in an airtight container for up to 2 days

VARIATIONS

■ **cranberry and fig** Substitute caster sugar with ⅓ cup firmly packed brown sugar. Omit sultanas; stir 1 cup coarsely chopped dried figs and ¼ cup dried cranberries into mixture before egg and milk are added.

■ **pineapple, lime and coconut** Omit sultanas; stir 1 cup coarsely chopped dried pineapple, ¼ cup toasted flaked coconut and 1 teaspoon finely grated lime rind into mixture before egg and milk are added.

jam roll

preparation time 20 minutes ▪ baking time 8 minutes
▪ serves 10

3 eggs, separated
½ cup (110g) caster sugar
¾ cup (110g) self-raising flour
2 tablespoons hot milk
¼ cup (110g) caster sugar, extra
½ cup (160g) jam, warmed

1 Position oven shelves; preheat oven to moderately hot. Grease 25cm x 30cm swiss roll tin; line base and short sides of tin with a strip of baking parchment, bringing paper 5cm over edges, grease paper.

2 Beat egg whites in small bowl with electric mixer until soft peaks form; gradually add sugar, 1 tablespoon at a time, beating until dissolved between additions.

3 With motor operating, add egg yolks, one at a time, beating until mixture is pale and thick; this will take about 10 minutes.

4 Meanwhile, sift flour three times onto baking parchment.

5 Pour hot milk down side of bowl; add triple-sifted flour. Working quickly, use plastic spatula to fold milk and flour through egg mixture. Pour mixture into prepared tin, gently spreading mixture evenly into corners.

6 Bake cake in moderately hot oven about 8 minutes or until top of cake feels soft and springy when touched lightly with fingertips.

7 Meanwhile, place a piece of baking parchment cut the same size as cake on board or bench; sprinkle evenly with extra sugar. When cooked, immediately turn cake onto sugared paper, quickly peeling away the lining paper. Working rapidly, use serrated knife to cut away crisp edges from all sides of cake.

8 Using hands, gently roll cake loosely from one of the short sides; unroll, spread evenly with jam.

9 Roll cake again, from same short side, by lifting paper and using it to guide the roll into shape. Either serve jam roll immediately with cream, or place onto wire rack to cool.

Also known as Swiss roll, or jelly roll in the United States, this filled and rolled sponge cake has long been a favourite in Britain, although its true origins are obscure. Quick and easy to make yet very impressive-looking, slices of the roll are good served warm or at room temperature with a dollop of whipped cream.

best-ever sponge cake

preparation time 25 minutes ▪ baking time 25 minutes ▪ serves 8

4 eggs
¾ cup (165g) caster sugar
1 cup (150g) self-raising flour
1 tablespoon cornflour
10g butter
⅓ cup (80ml) boiling water
⅓ cup (110g) lemon curd
¾ cup (180ml) double cream
1 tablespoon icing sugar

1 Position oven shelves; preheat oven to moderate. Grease two deep 20cm-round cake tins.

2 Beat eggs in large bowl with electric mixer until thick and foamy. Gradually add sugar, about a tablespoonful at a time, beating until sugar is dissolved between additions. Total beating time should be about 10 minutes.

3 Sift flour and cornflour together three times onto paper.

4 Sift flour mixture over egg mixture; using one hand like a rake, quickly and lightly fold and pull flour mixture through egg mixture, using the side of your hand as a scraper to make sure all the ingredients are combined.

5 Pour combined butter and the water down side of bowl; using one hand, fold through egg mixture. Pour mixture evenly into prepared tins, using metal spatula, spread mixture to edges of tins.

6 Bake sponges in moderate oven about 25 minutes. Immediately sponges are baked, turn onto wire racks covered with baking parchment; turn top-side up to cool.

7 Place one sponge on serving plate, spread with lemon curd and whipped cream. Top with remaining cake, dust with sifted icing sugar.

rich chocolate cake

preparation time 15 minutes ▨
baking time 1 hour 30 minutes
(plus cooling time) ▨ serves 8

185g butter
2 teaspoons vanilla extract
1¾ cups (385g) caster sugar
3 eggs
2 cups (300g) self-raising flour
⅔ cup (70g) cocoa powder
1 cup (250ml) water

chocolate icing
90g dark chocolate, chopped coarsely
30g butter
1 cup (160g) icing sugar
2 tablespoons hot water, approximately

1 Grease base and sides of deep
23cm-round cake tin; line base with
baking parchment.
2 Combine butter, extract, sugar, eggs,
flour, cocoa and the water in large bowl;
beat on low speed using electric mixer
until ingredients are combined. Increase
speed to medium; beat about 3 minutes
or until mixture is smooth and changed
in colour. Spread into prepared tin.
3 Bake in moderate oven 1½ hours.
Stand 5 minutes, then turn onto wire
rack to cool. Spread with chocolate icing.

▨ **chocolate icing** Melt chocolate and butter in medium bowl over hot water; gradually
stir in sifted icing sugar, then stir in enough of the water to mix to a spreadable consistency.

both butter and eggs should be at room temperature to avoid the mixture curdling ■ buy ready-mixed fruit, or mix your own to suit your taste; all fruit should be chopped to the size of a sultana ■ nuts can be added to the fruit mixture; 125g blanched almonds, chopped coarsely, is an ideal amount ■ you can use dark brown sugar for a more richly coloured cake ■ rum, brandy or your favourite liqueur can be substituted for the sherry ■ this cake can also be baked in a deep 22cm-round cake tin ■ cover cake loosely with foil during baking if it starts to overbrown ■ give cake quarter turns several times during baking so that it browns evenly ■ covered cake will take about 24 hours to cool to room temperature in tin ■ remove cake from tin by turning upside down onto worktop and carefully peeling paper away from sides but leaving base paper in place ■ to store, wrap cake tightly in cling film, then foil ■ wrapped cake will keep in a cool, dark place for about 3 months ■ cake can be frozen for up to 12 months

christmas cake

preparation time 30 minutes ■ baking time 3 hours ■ serves 36

250g butter, softened
1¼ cups (250g) firmly packed brown sugar
4 eggs
2 tablespoons orange marmalade
1.5kg (7¾ cups) mixed dried fruit
1½ cups (225g) plain flour
½ cup (75g) self-raising flour
2 teaspoons mixed spice
½ cup (125ml) sweet sherry
¼ cup (30g) blanched whole almonds
2 tablespoons sweet sherry, extra

1 Position oven shelves; preheat oven to slow. Line base and sides of deep 19cm-square cake tin with three thicknesses baking parchment, bringing paper 5cm above sides of tin.
2 Beat butter and sugar in small bowl with electric mixer until just combined; beat in eggs, one at a time, until just combined between additions. Mixture may curdle at this point but will come together later.
3 Scrape mixture into large bowl; add marmalade and fruit, mix thoroughly with one hand.
4 Sift flours and spice over mixture; add sherry, mix well.
5 Drop dollops of mixture into corners of tin to hold paper in position; spread remaining mixture into tin.
6 Drop cake tin from a height of about 15cm onto bench to settle mixture into pan and to break any large air bubbles; level surface of cake mixture with wet metal spatula, decorate top with almonds.
7 Bake cake in low oven about 3 hours. Remove cake from oven; brush top with extra sherry. Cover tin tightly with foil; cool cake in tin.

A popular combination of flavours makes this syrupy cake a safe bet for everybody. And, if you prefer to omit the syrup completely, the cake itself is still deliciously moist.

orange seed cake

preparation time 25 minutes ■
baking time 1 hour ■ serves 16

⅓ cup (50g) poppy seeds
¼ cup (60ml) milk
185g butter, softened
1 tablespoon finely grated orange rind
1 cup (220g) caster sugar
3 eggs
1½ cups (225g) self-raising flour
½ cup (75g) plain flour
½ cup (60g) ground almonds
½ cup (125ml) orange juice

orange syrup
1 cup (220g) caster sugar
⅔ cup (160ml) orange juice
⅓ cup (80ml) water

1 Position oven shelves; preheat oven to moderate. Grease deep 22cm-round cake tin; line base and side with baking parchment.
2 Combine seeds and milk in small bowl; stand 20 minutes.
3 Meanwhile, beat butter, rind and sugar in small bowl with electric mixer until light and fluffy; beat in eggs, one at a time, until just combined between additions.
4 Transfer mixture to large bowl; using wooden spoon, stir in flours, ground almonds, juice and poppy seed mixture. Spread mixture into prepared tin.
5 Bake cake in moderate oven about 1 hour. Stand cake 5 minutes then turn onto wire rack over tray; turn top-side up, pour hot syrup over hot cake. Return any syrup that drips onto tray to jug; pour over cake.

■ orange syrup Using a wooden spoon, stir combined ingredients in small saucepan over heat, without boiling, until sugar dissolves; bring to a boil. Reduce heat; simmer, uncovered, without stirring, 2 minutes. Pour syrup into heatproof jug.

ginger cake

preparation time 15 minutes ▪ baking time 1 hour 30 minutes ▪ serves 24

1½ cups (300g) firmly packed
brown sugar
1½ cups (225g) plain flour
1½ cups (225g) self-raising flour
½ teaspoon bicarbonate of soda
1 tablespoon ground ginger
2 teaspoons ground cinnamon
1 teaspoon ground nutmeg
250g butter, softened
2 eggs
1 cup (250ml) buttermilk
½ cup (175g) golden syrup

lemon frosting
60g butter, softened
2 teaspoons finely grated lemon rind
2 tablespoons lemon juice
2 cups (320g) icing sugar mixture

1 Position oven shelves; preheat oven to moderately slow. Grease deep 23cm-square cake tin; line base with baking parchment.

2 Sift dry ingredients into large bowl of electric mixer, add remaining ingredients. Beat mixture on low speed until ingredients are combined, then beat on medium speed until mixture is smooth and changed to a paler colour. Using metal spatula, spread mixture into prepared tin.

3 Bake cake in moderately slow oven about 1½ hours. Stand cake 10 minutes, turn onto wire rack, turn top-side up to cool. Spread cold cake with lemon frosting.

▪ **lemon frosting** Using wooden spoon, beat butter and rind together in small bowl; gradually beat in juice and icing sugar.

glossary

almonds flat, pointed-ended nuts with pitted brown shell enclosing a creamy white kernel covered by a brown skin.

blanched nuts have brown skins removed.

ground almonds nuts are powdered to a coarse flour texture, for use in baking or as a thickening agent.

aubergine also known as eggplant.

baking parchment also known as silicon paper or non-stick baking paper; not to be confused with greaseproof or waxed paper. Used to line tins before cooking, baking and also to make piping bags.

barley a nutritious grain used in soups and stews as well as in whiskey- and beer-making.

beef

brisket from the under section of the forequarter and ribs, rolled and secured with string or netting.

chuck steak from the neck area; can be used as one piece or as steak.

bicarbonate of soda also known as baking soda.

breadcrumbs

fresh bread, usually white, processed into crumbs.

packaged prepared fine-textured but crunchy white breadcrumbs.

stale made by blending or processing 1- or 2-day-old bread.

butter use salted or unsalted (sweet) butter.

buttermilk sold alongside fresh milk products in supermarkets and is commercially made, by a method similar to yogurt. Despite the implication of its name, it is low in fat and is a good substitute for dairy products such as cream or sour cream, good in baking and in salad dressings.

caraway seeds a member of the parsley family; available as seeds or ground and can be used in sweet and savoury dishes.

celeriac tuberous root with brown skin, white flesh and a celery-like flavour.

cheese

cheddar use a firm, good-tasting cheese. We used a variety containing 33% fat.

parmesan also known as parmigiano; a hard, grainy cow's-milk cheese.

ricotta soft white cow milk cheese; roughly translates as 'cooked again'. It's made from whey, a by-product of other cheese making, to which fresh milk and acid are added. Ricotta is a sweet, moist cheese with a fat content of

around 8.5% and a slightly grainy texture.

chicken, breast fillet breast halved, skinned and boned.

chilli generally the smaller the chilli, the hotter it is. Use rubber gloves when seeding and chopping fresh chillies to prevent burning your skin.

red thai small, medium hot and bright red in colour.

cinnamon dried inner bark of the shoots of the cinnamon tree.

cocoa powder also known as unsweetened cocoa.

coconut, desiccated unsweetened, concentrated, dried finely shredded coconut.

cornflour also known as cornstarch; used as a thickening agent in cooking.

courgette also known as zucchini; small green, yellow or white members of the squash family having edible flowers.

cream fresh pouring cream; has a minimum fat content of 35%.

whipping (thickened) has a minimum fat content of 35% and includes a thickener.

cumin also known as zeera; related to the parsley family. Has a spicy, nutty flavour. Available in seed form or dried and ground.

currants tiny, almost-black raisins so-named after a grape variety that originated in Corinth, Greece.

curry powder

powder a blend of various ground spices, available mild or hot; may include chilli, cumin, cinnamon, coriander, fennel, fenugreek, mace, cardamom and turmeric.

custard powder packaged powdered mixture of starch (wheat or corn), artificial flavouring and colouring.

flour

plain also known as all-purpose; unbleached wheat flour.

self-raising all-purpose plain flour with baking powder added in the proportion of 1 cup flour to 2 teaspoons baking powder.

fennel also known as finocchio or anise; a crunchy green vegetable slightly resembling celery; also sometimes the name given to the dried seeds of the plant, which have a stronger licorice flavour.

gelatine we used powdered gelatine; also available in sheet form known as leaf gelatine.

ginger

fresh also known as green or root ginger; the thick gnarled root of a tropical plant.

ground also known as powdered ginger. A flavouring used in puddings and cakes; cannot be substituted for fresh ginger.

jam also known as preserve or conserve.

lamb

leg from the hindquarter.

neck chop we used 'best' neck chops.

rack row of cutlets.

shank forequarter leg.

lamb's lettuce also known as lamb's tongue, corn salad or mâche, it has clusters of tiny, tender, nutty-tasting leaves.

lemon curd also known as lemon cheese, lemon butter or lemon spread; a creamed mixture made from lemon juice and/or rind, egg yolks, butter and sugar, in varying proportions.

lentils (red, brown, yellow) dried pulses often identified by and named after their colour. French green lentils are green-blue, tiny lentils with a nutty, earthy flavour and a hardy nature that allows them to be rapidly cooked without disintegrating. They are a local cousin to the famous (and expensive) French lentils du puy.

marmalade a preserve, usually based on citrus fruit and its rind.

miso paste is grouped into two main categories – red and white, although the 'red' is dark brown in colour and the 'white' is more the colour of weak tea. Made in Japan, miso is a paste made from cooked, mashed, salted and fermented soy beans, and is a common ingredient in soups, sauces and dressings.

mixed dried fruit a combination of sultanas, raisins, currants, mixed peel and cherries.

mixed spice a classic mixture generally containing caraway, allspice, coriander, cumin, nutmeg and ginger, although cinnamon and other spices can be added. It is used with fruit and in cakes.

mushrooms

button small, cultivated white mushrooms having a delicate, subtle flavour.

dried porcini also known as cèpes. Has a strong, rich, nutty flavour; must be rehydrated before use.

mustard

dijon a pale brown, distinctively flavoured, fairly mild French mustard.

wholegrain also known as seeded. A French-style coarse-grain mustard made from crushed mustard seeds and dijon-style French mustard.

oil

olive made from ripened olives. Extra virgin and virgin are the first and second press, respectively, of the olives and are therefore considered the best while extra light or light is diluted and refers to taste not fat levels.

vegetable oils sourced from plants rather than animal fats.

onions

brown and white are inter-changeable. Their pungent flesh adds flavour to a vast range of dishes.

spring also known as green or scallion; have crisp, narrow green-leafed tops.

red also known as spanish, red spanish or bermuda onion; a sweet-flavoured, large, purple-red onion.

shallots also called french shallots, golden shallots or eschalots. Small, elongated, brown-skinned members of the onion family.

parsley, flat-leaf also known as continental parsley or italian parsley.

pecan nuts native to the united states and now grown locally; golden-brown, buttery and rich. Good in savoury as well as sweet dishes; especially good in salads.

pepper also known as capsicum or bell pepper. Seeds and membranes should be discarded before use. Also available char-grilled, packed in oil, in jars.

pine nuts also known as pignoli; not really nuts, but small, cream-coloured kernels from the cones of some pine trees.

poppy seeds possess a nutty, slightly sweet flavour and a dark blue-grey colour.

port a rich, sweet dessert wine fortified with brandy.

prawns also known as shrimp.

puff pastry, ready-rolled packaged sheets of frozen puff pastry, available from supermarkets.

pumpkin also known as squash.

raisins dried sweet grapes (traditionally muscatel grapes).

redcurrant jelly a preserve made from red currants; it is an imported product available from some supermarkets and delicatessens.

sambal oelek also ulek or olek; Indonesian in origin, this is a salty paste made from ground chillies and vinegar.

sauces

cranberry a packaged product made of cranberries cooked in sugar syrup.

sweet chilli a comparatively mild, Thai-type sauce made from red chillies, sugar, garlic and vinegar.

tabasco brand name of an extremely fiery sauce made from vinegar, hot red peppers and salt.

worcestershire a thin, dark-brown spicy sauce used as a seasoning.

sherry fortified wine consumed as an apertif or used in cooking. Sold as fino (light, dry), amontillado (medium sweet, dark) and oloroso (full-bodied, very dark).

spinach also known as english spinach and, incorrectly, silver beet. Baby spinach leaves are best eaten raw in salads.

split peas also known as field peas; green or yellow pulse grown especially for drying and split in half along a centre seam.

sponge-finger biscuits also known as savoy biscuits, lady's fingers or savoiardi; they are Italian-style crisp fingers made from sponge-cake mixture.

stock 1 cup (250ml) stock is equivalent to 1 cup (250ml) water plus 1 crumbled stock cube (or 1 teaspoon crumbled stock powder).

sugar

brown a soft, finely granulated sugar retaining molasses for colour and flavour.

caster also known as superfine or finely granulated table sugar.

icing also known as confectioners' or powdered sugar.

white also known as crystal or granulated table sugar.

sultanas dried grapes, also known as golden raisins.

sweet potato fleshy white root vegetable.

swiss roll tin (also known as a jelly-roll pan) measures 26cm x 32cm in area; its slightly raised sides (averaging 2cm in height) help contain the mixture being baked in it, preventing the sponge from rising. Often the baked item is removed from the tin and rolled while still hot and malleable, then later unrolled, spread with a sweet or savoury filling, and rolled again before slicing.

vanilla

bean dried long, thin pod from a tropical golden orchid; the tiny black seeds inside the bean are used to impart a luscious vanilla flavour in baking and desserts.

extract made by extracting the flavour from the vanilla bean pod; the pods are soaked, usually in alcohol, to capture the authentic flavour.

vinegar

cider (apple cider) made from fermented apples.

malt (brown) made from fermented malt and beech shavings.

red wine based on fermented red wine.

white wine made from white wine.

walnuts wrinkled, cream-coloured nuts with brown skin, with two distinct halves.

yogurt, low-fat we used yogurt with a fat content of less than 0.2%.

conversion charts

Measures

The cup and spoon measurements used in this book are metric: one measuring cup holds approximately 250ml; one metric tablespoon holds 20ml; one metric teaspoon holds 5ml.

All cup and spoon measurements are level. The most accurate way of measuring dry ingredients is to weigh them. When measuring liquids, use a clear glass or plastic jug with metric markings. We used large eggs with an average weight of 60g.

WARNING This book contains recipes for dishes made with raw or lightly cooked eggs. These should be avoided by vulnerable people such as pregnant and nursing mothers, invalids, the elderly, babies and young children.

Dry measures

metric	imperial
15g	½oz
30g	1oz
60g	2oz
90g	3oz
125g	4oz (¼lb)
155g	5oz
185g	6oz
220g	7oz
250g	8oz (½lb)
280g	9oz
315g	10oz
345g	11oz
375g	12oz (¾lb)
410g	13oz
440g	14oz
470g	15oz
500g	16oz (1lb)
750g	24oz (1½lb)
1kg	32oz (2lb)

Liquid measures

metric	imperial
30ml	1 fl oz
60ml	2 fl oz
100ml	3 fl oz
125ml	4 fl oz
150ml	5 fl oz (¼ pint/1 gill)
190ml	6 fl oz
250ml	8 fl oz
300ml	10 fl oz (½pt)
500ml	16 fl oz
600ml	20 fl oz (1 pint)
1000ml (1 litre)	1¾pints

Length measures

metric	imperial
3mm	⅛in
6mm	¼in
1cm	½in
2cm	¾in
2.5cm	1in
5cm	2in
6cm	2½in
8cm	3in
10cm	4in
13cm	5in
15cm	6in
18cm	7in
20cm	8in
23cm	9in
25cm	10in
28cm	11in
30cm	12in (1ft)

Oven temperatures

These oven temperatures are only a guide for conventional ovens. For fan-assisted ovens, check the manufacturer's manual.

	°C (Celcius)	°F (Fahrenheit)	gas mark
Very low	120	250	½
Low	150	275-300	1-2
Moderately low	170	325	3
Moderate	180	350-375	4-5
Moderately hot	200	400	6
Hot	220	425-450	7-8
Very hot	240	475	9

index

ARE YOU MISSING SOME COOKBOOKS?

The Australian Women's Weekly Cookbooks are available from bookshops, cookshops, supermarkets and other stores all over the world. You can also buy direct from the publisher, using the order form below.

TITLE	RRP	QTY	TITLE	RRP	QTY
100 Fast Fillets	£6.99		Grills	£6.99	
A Taste of Chocolate	£6.99		Indian Cooking Class	£6.99	
After Work Fast	£6.99		Japanese Cooking Class	£6.99	
Beginners Cooking Class	£6.99		Just For One	£6.99	
Beginners Thai	£6.99		Just For Two	£6.99	
Best Food Fast	£6.99		Kids' Birthday Cakes	£6.99	
Breads & Muffins	£6.99		Kids Cooking	£6.99	
Brunches, Lunches & Treats	£6.99		Kids' Cooking Step-by-Step	£6.99	
Cafe Classics	£6.99		Low-carb, Low-fat	£6.99	
Cafe Favourites	£6.99		Low-fat Food for Life	£6.99	
Cakes Bakes & Desserts	£6.99		Low-fat Meals in Minutes	£6.99	
Cakes Biscuits & Slices	£6.99		Main Course Salads	£6.99	
Cakes Cooking Class	£6.99		Mexican	£6.99	
Caribbean Cooking	£6.99		Middle Eastern Cooking Class	£6.99	
Casseroles	£6.99		Mince in Minutes	£6.99	
Casseroles & Slow-Cooked Classics	£6.99		Moroccan & the Foods of North Africa	£6.99	
Cheap Eats	£6.99		Muffins, Scones & Breads	£6.99	
Cheesecakes: baked and chilled	£6.99		New Casseroles	£6.99	
Chicken	£6.99		New Curries	£6.99	
Chicken Meals in Minutes	£6.99		New Finger Food	£6.99	
Chinese and the foods of Thailand, Vietnam, Malaysia & Japan	£6.99		New French Food	£6.99	
			New Salads	£6.99	
Chinese Cooking Class	£6.99		Party Food and Drink	£6.99	
Christmas Cooking	£6.99		Pasta Meals in Minutes	£6.99	
Chocs & Treats	£6.99		Potatoes	£6.99	
Cocktails	£6.99		Quick & Simple Cooking (Apr 08)	£6.99	
Cookies & Biscuits	£6.99		Rice & Risotto	£6.99	
Cooking Class Cake Decorating	£6.99		Sauces Salsas & Dressings	£6.99	
Cupcakes & Fairycakes	£6.99		Sensational Stir-Fries	£6.99	
Detox	£6.99		Simple Healthy Meals	£6.99	
Dinner Lamb	£6.99		Simple Starters Mains & Puds	£6.99	
Easy Comfort Food (May 08)	£6.99		Soup	£6.99	
Easy Curry	£6.99		Stir-fry	£6.99	
Easy Midweek Meals	£6.99		Superfoods for Exam Success	£6.99	
Easy Spanish-Style	£6.99		Tapas Mezze Antipasto & other bites	£6.99	
Food for Fit and Healthy Kids	£6.99		Thai Cooking Class	£6.99	
Foods of the Mediterranean	£6.99		Traditional Italian	£6.99	
Foods That Fight Back	£6.99		Vegetarian Meals in Minutes	£6.99	
Fresh Food Fast	£6.99		Vegie Food	£6.99	
Fresh Food for Babies & Toddlers	£6.99		Wicked Sweet Indulgences	£6.99	
Good Food for Babies & Toddlers	£6.99		Wok Meals in Minutes	£6.99	
Great Kids' Cakes (May 08)	£6.99				
Greek Cooking Class	£6.99		TOTAL COST:	£	

Mr/Mrs/Ms _____

Address _____

_____ Postcode _____

Day time phone _____ Email* (optional) _____

I enclose my cheque/money order for £ _____

or please charge £ _____

to my: ☐ Access ☐ Mastercard ☐ Visa ☐ Diners Club

Card number | | | | | | | | | | | | | | | | |

Expiry date _____ 3 digit security code *(found on reverse of card)* _____

Cardholder's name_____ Signature _____

* By including your email address, you consent to receipt of any email regarding this magazine, and other emails which inform you of ACP's other publications, products, services and events, and to promote third party goods and services you may be interested in.

ACP BOOKS

General manager Christine Whiston
Test kitchen food director Pamela Clark
Editorial director Susan Tomnay
Creative director Hieu Chi Nguyen
Director of sales Brian Cearnes
Marketing manager Bridget Cody
Business analyst Rebecca Varela
Operations manager David Scotto
International rights enquiries Laura Bamford
lbamford@acpuk.com

ACP Books are published by ACP Magazines a division of PBL Media Pty Limited
Group publisher, Women's lifestyle
Pat Ingram
Director of sales, Women's lifestyle
Lynette Phillips
Commercial manager, Women's lifestyle
Seymour Cohen
Marketing director, Women's lifestyle
Matthew Dominello
Public relations manager, Women's lifestyle
Hannah Deveraux
Creative director, Events, Women's lifestyle
Luke Bonnano
Research Director, Women's lifestyle
Justin Stone
ACP Magazines, Chief Executive officer
Scott Lorson
PBL Media, Chief Executive officer
Ian Law

Produced by ACP Books, Sydney.
Published by ACP Books, a division of ACP Magazines Ltd, 54 Park St, Sydney; GPO Box 4088, Sydney, NSW 2001.
phone (02) 9282 8618 fax (02) 9267 9438.
acpbooks@acpmagazines.com.au
www.acpbooks.com.au
Printed and bound in China.

Australia Distributed by Network Services, phone +61 2 9282 8777 fax +61 2 9264 3278
networkweb@networkservicescompany.com.au
United Kingdom Distributed by Australian Consolidated Press (UK), phone (01604) 642 200 fax (01604) 642 300
books@acpuk.com
New Zealand Distributed by Netlink Distribution Company, phone (9) 366 9966 ask@ndc.co.nz
South Africa Distributed by PSD Promotions, phone (27 11) 392 6065/6/7 fax (27 11) 392 6079/80
orders@psdprom.co.za
Canada Distributed by Publishers Group Canada phone (800) 663 5714 fax (800) 565 3770
service@raincoast.com